Contents

Acknowledgements

We are most grateful for the numerous occasions when Peter Hancock has helped us in the preparation of the programs contained in the Beginner's Guide. We are also grateful to Leslie Smith for his advice throughout the project and to David Cairns for his invaluable assistance in modifying the programs for the Apple Macintosh and IBM PC versions. We are also grateful to the many undergraduate and post-graduate students, who freely gave us their views on early versions of this guide.

The Beginner's Guide was developed from work originally funded by the UGC / Computer Board Computers in Teaching Initiative, Grant Number C97/020/01, awarded to W.A. Phillips and L.S. Smith, at the Centre for Cognitive and Computational Neuroscience, University of Stirling.

The programs were designed by Gerry Orchard and Bill Phillips, and all were written by Gerry Orchard. The simulation for Position Invariance (Chapter 9) was developed from an original program written by Geoffrey Hinton. The simulation for self-organizing feature maps (Chapter 8) was developed from an original program written by Peter Hancock.

The layout of the Beginner's Guide was designed by Jennifer Cleland and Gerry Orchard.

Finally, we thank Jennifer Cleland and Rena Phillips, for without their patient understanding and moral support this guide would not have been completed.

1

Overview of the Guide

This guide is a brief introduction to neural computation. The intention is to give the user a feel for the area, and a general understanding of the basic functions, architecture, and algorithms for broad classes of neurocomputational systems. Throughout the text references to work by some of the principle researchers will be given, particularly the work of McClelland, Rumelhart and the PDP research group (McClelland & Rumelhart, 1986; Rumelhart & McClelland, 1986) for those who wish to explore in greater depth. The objective of this guide is to provide simple examples of neural computation and the parallel distributed processing approaches. You will probably already be aware of how radically the ideas embodied in neural computation are affecting the way we re-assess old problems and think about new ones. It is useful therefore to understand these ideas from a broad conceptual angle even though precise mathematical understanding of exactly how individual algorithms operate may not come easily.

The chapters are arranged roughly in order of complexity and the naive user is advised to follow the programs in numerical order. Most of the chapters have more than one program and where this is this case the first program is primarily a demonstration where input and some other variables are controlled by the program rather than the user. Interaction with the net is restricted and the procedure is rather pedantic as the main purpose of the demonstration simulation is to provide examples of the net's characteristics.

Later simulations in each chapter allow users to interact freely with the net, changing input and appropriate variables to suit their needs.

Exercises to guide users and help exploration of the net are provided for each module, as are references for further study.

Separate versions of simulations for the Beginner's Guide are available; for the Acorn Archimedes, the Apple Macintosh and the IBM PC family of microcomputers. All versions require high resolution graphic capabilities and the provision of a mouse. Further hardware specifications are given in Chapter Two.

Chapter Two: Getting Started

This chapter gives you guidelines for making backup copies of your floppy disks and the hard disk installation procedure, together with instructions for using the neural nets simulations.

Chapter Three: Introduction to basic concepts

The module contains a program demonstrating what neurocomputation and parallel distributed processing (PDP) are and explaining some of the advantages and characteristics of neurocomputational systems. The text introduces the elementary components on which neural computation is based, the neuron, its structure and activation, and the way in which individual neurons are connected to each other to form several nets. The architecture of some of these neural nets and the way in which information is represented and processed within them is briefly outlined before introducing the overall concept of learning in neural nets. We then outline some of the computational, biological and psychological perspectives on neural net research.

Chapter Four: Lateral Inhibition

The programs within this chapter simulate some of the lateral inhibitory processes important in early visual processing. Two forms of architecture, feedforward and recurrent, are covered. The simulations also introduce the user to the computer interface and the symbol system used for input, output, unit activation levels, excitation and inhibition throughout the package and the techniques for using the mouse to change parameters. All users should work through Program Two of this chapter at least well enough to learn these general aspects of program use.

Chapter Five: Auto-association

Auto-associators are simple neural nets that have the capacity to store patterns as distributed representations. The patterns can be recalled using cues, or parts of the pattern, even when the cue contains errors. Auto-associative nets can also derive prototypical patterns that underlie a number of similar patterns.

Four different Hebbian learning rules (algorithms) for changing the strengths of the connections (synapses) between units are introduced. The distributed memory of a pattern may differ according to which of these learning rules is applied. Each learning rule produces a different pattern of connection strengths between units, with corresponding differences in the net's performance.

The Delta rule, also modelled closely on work by McClelland and Rumelhart (1985), is introduced. A pattern is learned by changing the connection strengths (weights) between units using an error term. The difference between the desired output of the net (i.e., the pattern it produces) and the actual output are computed, and the strengths of connections between units are altered to reduce the difference (error). The procedure cycles until the error is reduced to a minimum.

Chapter Six: Pattern Association

Pattern associators are neural nets that can be taught to associate one pattern with another, a sort of simple stimulus-response mechanism, where if one pattern is presented to the system it responds by producing its associate. This chapter, like the chapter on auto-association, introduces two versions of pattern associators; those using Hebbian learning rules and those using the Delta rule.

Chapter Seven: Backpropagation

Nets with a single-layer of connections cannot solve some simple logical problems e.g., the exclusive-or problem. Nets with three layers of units and two layers of connections are able to do this because the middle layer can learn to code the input appropriately. This is achieved by successively feeding back between layers the difference between desired and actual output (i.e., back-propagation of the Delta rule).

The more complex weight change procedure of backpropagation allows it to learn mappings that the simpler procedures cannot.

Chapter Eight: Competitive Learning

Competitive learning is a system which organizes itself so as to develop its own representations of the patterns it experiences. It does this by using inhibitory connections between units in the same layer and by using specifically designed procedures for learning. This is sometimes described as "feature discovery" (Rumelhart & Zipser, 1986). Competitive learning represents another class of multi-layer network architectures and algorithms capable of detecting regularities in the input.

Chapter Nine: Position Invariance

The final chapter shows one way in which the difficult problem of perceptual invariance could be solved using a neural net. It might not appear obvious at first, but recognizing an object seen at any location within the visual field is a complex problem for neural systems and we do not yet fully understand how biological systems do it. Hinton's (1981a) description of how this might be achieved forms the basis of the simulation.

2

Getting Started

The Beginner's Guide simulations are available for the Acorn Archimedes, the Apple Macintosh and the IBM PC family of microcomputers. All versions require a high resolution monitor (colour for Archimedes and PC versions) and a mouse. The three versions have the same content though their appearance will vary depending on the type of monitor, and control of the programs will depend on the type of mouse. Each version is described separately in the following sections.

Please read the ReadMe file for recent updates or load the ReadMe.Txt file into your word processor.

Floppy disks

Three disks are provided for each version. All disks are formatted for normal double density, 80 track. The program modules on each floppy disk are:

Neural Nets 1:	Introduction (Chapter 3) Lateral Inhibition (Chapter 4) Competitive Learning (Chapter 8)
Neural Nets 2:	Auto association (Chapter 5)
Neural Nets 3:	Pattern Association (Chapter 6) Backpropagation (Chapter 7) Position Invariance (Chapter 9)

PLEASE MAKE BACKUP COPIES OF YOUR FLOPPY DISKS BEFORE PROCEEDING FURTHER.

Acorn Archimedes

Hardware configuration

The simulation runs on any Acorn Archimedes microcomputer and requires a colour monitor for optimal display of the programs. The more recent Archimedes computers use the RISCOS operating system, earlier versions may be using the ARTHUR operating system if they have not been upgraded. The Beginner's Guide runs on both operating systems.

Formatting and making backup copies of your floppy disks

Archimedes running the RISCOS operating system: insert the blank disk in the drive. Use the middle mouse button to select the floppy disk drive icon on the left-hand side of the screen. Select Format, select D: 800K Old Map and follow the instructions on the screen.

Ensure that the write-protect tab on each Neural Net disk is ON.The simplest and quickest way of making a backup is by using the operating system command BACKUP.

Press the F12 function key, type BACKUP 0 0 Q at the * prompt and then follow the instructions on the screen.

Hard disk installation

Please ensure that the hard disk has at least 1.5 Megabytes of free space available if you wish to install the programs.

Insert Neural Nets 1 into the drive, select the floppy disk and double click on HDINSTALL. The program will automatically create a directory called "NNets" on the root directory. After a set of files has been copied from Neural Nets 1 the program will prompt you to replace it with Neural Nets 2 and then Neural Nets 3. After you have been notified that the Beginner's Guide has been successfully installed you will be returned to the desktop.

Running the neural net simulations

Hard Disk. Double click on the NNets directory icon then double click on the !NNets icon. The Beginner's Guide menu will be presented. Move the pointer to the appropriate module title and then click the left-hand mouse button and follow the menu prompts.

Floppy Disk. Select the disk you require, double click on the !NNets icon and The Beginner's Guide menu will be presented. The program will prompt you to change disks when necessary.

Using the mouse and selecting items

The Archimedes mouse contains three buttons but the simulations are controlled by the left-hand and centre mouse buttons only. The pointer is usually restricted within an area that determines an appropriate range of options for the task in hand. To select one item at a time: e.g. the choice of modules from the main menu: move the mouse so that the pointer is inside the selected box and then click the left-hand button. To select several items or to exit from an option: e.g. when inputting a pattern, select each item by clicking the left-hand button and when selection is complete click the centre button to exit.

Apple Macintosh

Hardware configuration

The simulation will run on any Apple Macintosh microcomputer though performance is greatly improved on Apple Macs with faster microprocessors such as the Mac SE range.

Formatting and making backup copies of your floppy disks

Ensure that the write-protect tab on each Neural Net disk is ON. Format three disks by inserting each Mac disk in the floppy drive and following the instructions on the screen. Entitle the three disks Neural Nets 1, Neural Nets 2, Neural Nets 3. Be sure to copy the titles exactly.

Insert the original Beginner's Guide Neural Nets 1 in the drive, select File-Eject from the control panel, insert the backup floppy, then drag the Neural Nets 1 icon onto the backup floppy. Follow the instructions on the screen. Repeat for the other two backup copies.

Hard disk installation

Please ensure that the hard disk has at least 1.5 Megabytes of free space available if you wish to install the programs.

Create a new folder entitled NNets on the root directory or anywhere else. Copy the contents of each Neural Net disk into this folder (select all and drag).

Running the neural net simulations

Hard Disk. Double click on the NNets icon to open the folder, then double click on the !NNets icon. The Beginner's Guide menu will be presented. Move the pointer to the appropriate module title, click the mouse button and follow the menu prompts.

Floppy Disk. Select the disk you require, double click on the !NNets icon and The Beginner's Guide menu will be presented. The program will prompt you to change disks when necessary.

Using the mouse and selecting items

The Apple Macintosh mouse has only one button and a design philosophy which prevents the pointer from being restricted. Control of the programs requires careful positioning of the pointer, alertness to onscreen messages and the use of single or double clicks on the mouse button.

To select one item at a time: e.g. the choice of modules from the main menu: move the mouse so that the pointer is inside the selected box and then click the button. To select several items or to exit from an option: e.g. when inputting a pattern, select each item by clicking the button and when selection is complete double click the button to exit. Prompts will be displayed in the control panel at the top of the screen, often accompanied by a beep to draw your attention.

IBM PC family

Hardware configuration

The neural net simulations require the following hardware configuration:
Computer: IBM PC, XT, AT, PS/2 models or 100% compatibles running under MS-Dos. Performance of the simulations is greatly improved on machines with faster microprocessors (ideally 80286 and above).
Monitor: IBM 8513, IBM 8514, EGA, VGA, Super VGA, MultiSync.
Mouse: Bus or serial mouse.

Formatting and making backup copies of your floppy disks

The IBM PC version is available on both $5^1/_4$ and $3^1/_2$ disks. Given the variety of methods for formatting and backup, users are advised to consult their manufacturer's manual for relevant procedures.

Hard disk installation

Please ensure that the hard disk has at least 1.5 Megabytes of free space available if you wish to install the programs.

Insert Neural Nets 1 into the drive. Type HDINSTALL at the floppy drive prompt. The program will automatically create a directory called "NNets" on the C drive (C: \NNets). After a set of files has been copied from Neural Nets 1 the program will prompt you to replace it with Neural Nets 2 and then Neural Nets 3. After you have been notified that the Beginner's Guide has been successfully installed you will be returned to the desktop.

Running the neural net simulations

Hard Disk. Move to the NNets directory (C: \NNets). Type NNets followed by a return (enter) to initialize the programs, then type NN followed by a return and the Beginner's Guide will be presented.

Floppy Disk. Select the disk you require and place it in the drive. If you have a hard disk or more than one floppy drive select the appropriate floppy drive by typing the drive letter followed by a colon (e.g., A:). Type NNets followed by a return (enter) to initialize the programs, then type NN followed by a return and the Beginner's Guide menu will be presented. The program will prompt you to change disks when necessary.

Controlling the programs (all versions)

There are two types of mouse-operated menus, one for text, and one for the simulations. They are referred to as "Control panels" throughout this manual.

Control of the text

At the top of the screen you will see a narrow light-grey strip with three panels labelled *Quit*, *Review*, and *Continue*.

Quit produces a window with three further options:

i. *Yes* returns to the main menu.
ii. *Cancel* returns you to the program or back to the menu.
iii. *Continue* - to next program.

Review If there is more than one page of text takes you back one page.
Continue takes you forward one page or into the neural net simulation.

Control of the neural net simulations

At the top of the screen you will see the main control panel, a wider light grey strip with a number of panels labelled with different control functions (see Figure 2.1). One of these (*Options*) is constant across programs. The others vary from program to program and will be specified for each program separately.

If you select *Options* a second control panel, the "Options Panel", will appear on the screen (see Figure 2.1). The *Quit* and *Continue* selections remain constant across programs, but others vary.

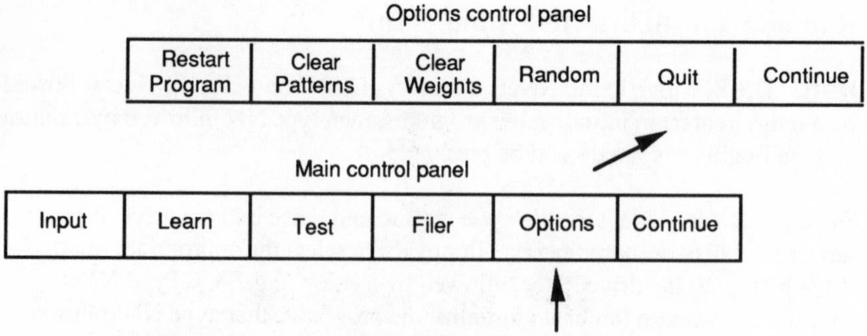

Figure 2.1. An example of the neural net simulation control panels

Clear, *Clear Weights* or *Reset Weights*, clears all variables but leaves the pattern set intact.
Clear Patterns clears all patterns and data but retains other variables.
Restart Module clears all the variables in the program and restarts it.
Quit is the same as for text control.
Continue returns you to the main control panel (see Figure 2.1).

3

Introduction to Basic Concepts

This guide is for beginners in three senses. It is a guide by beginners, for beginners, to an enterprise that is just beginning. During the 1980s many computer scientists, neuroscientists, and psychologists began work on neural computing, and the ideas and applications are being developed rapidly in many different directions. This general area of research is also referred to as connectionism, parallel distributed processing, associative memory, and computational neuroscience, and each of these terms captures some part of the spirit of the enterprise.

The central aim of this enterprise can be stated simply. It is to discover how neural systems acquire and use knowledge. Until recently the way that mental functions arise from neural activity was a complete mystery. Now computer simulations of neural networks are beginning to resolve part of that mystery. What is becoming clear is how some basic computational abilities can arise from the collective activity of populations of neurons. It must be emphasized, however, that these basic abilities are very different from the abilities on which all conventional computers are based. Brains and conventional computers are designed on very different principles, and have very different abilities and limitations. This chapter tries to make clear what those differences are, and why they are important.

An understanding of how brains compute would suggest the design for a new family of computers because brains can do many things that conventional computers cannot. This helps justify investment in this research, but our main motivation remains that of trying to discover how our minds are related to our brains and to the world in which we find ourselves.

Nervous systems, computation, and psychology are all such vast subjects that it is first necessary to indicate the areas within those subjects with which we will be most concerned. Our main focus is on systems capable of intelligent adaptation, i.e., systems that can acquire knowledge about their environment from experience, and then use that knowledge to guide action. Perception, memory, learning and action in the real world are therefore the psychological functions whose computational bases we seek. From a biological perspective, the cerebral cortex is the part of the brain specifically designed to provide 12 intelligent adaptation. An understanding of cortical structure and function is therefore one of the ultimate goals.

Structure and function in neural nets: A simple outline

Neural nets consist of many elementary processors that integrate the information they receive from other elements or from the environment, and then send the result to other elementary processors or to effectors such as the motor system. Input, internal processing, and output all involve the cooperative activity of large numbers of elements. Thus information is contained in patterns of activity that are distributed across many elements and that change from moment to moment through their many simultaneous interactions.

In this section we will outline the elementary processing components of neural systems, and describe some simple patterns of inter-connection, or connection architectures. We will then outline the ways in which these structures represent, process, and acquire information.

The elementary components

We will first describe the elements of biological nervous systems and then the corresponding elements of neural computers. The nerve cell, or neuron, is the fundamental element of all biological nervous systems. In simple creatures, such as slugs, there may be only a few thousand neurons, but in mammalian brains there are many more, and anatomists estimate that in the human brain there may be as many as approximately 10^{12} neurons (i.e. a million million). Although there are various shapes and sizes of neurons, there are basic features common to all neurons in all species. The most important is a cell membrane that contains many microscopic channels that allow electrically charged particles to flow in or out of the cell. The degree to which these channels are open or closed is highly sensitive to a variety of factors and in particular to the inputs received from other neurons. As a consequence the extent to which the cell is electrically charged is in a constant state of flux that is exquisitely sensitive to its ever changing input.

Figure 3.1 shows the structure of a pyramidal cell, which is the most common kind of cortical neuron. Three main parts of a neuron are the dendritic tree, the cell body, and the axon. The dendrites receive signals from other neurons. The degree to which the cell body itself is electrically charged depends upon all these separate inputs, and this summary state determines the signal that will be sent along the axon to all the other neurons to which it is connected. Some inputs are excitatory and others are inhibitory, and it is the overall balance between excitatory and inhibitory inputs that determine what signal will finally be transmitted. If the cell is strongly inhibited then no signal will be sent. Otherwise, a signal is transmitted along the axon that takes the form of brief pulses, or spikes, that are sent more frequently when the cell is more excited. The highest frequency with which spikes can be transmitted is roughly 500 spikes per second, but is usually much less. Thus neuronal output varies from 0 to about 500 spikes per second. Unless specifically excited or inhibited neurons show a "spontaneous" activity of roughly 10 spikes per second.

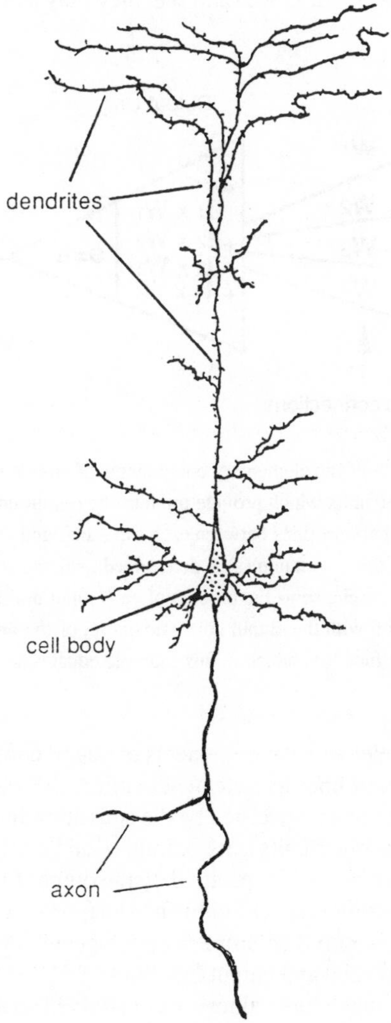

Figure 3.1. Outline sketch of a cortical pyramidal cell

Lastly, there are the synapses. These are the tiny local regions where signals are transmitted from the axon of one neuron to the receptive regions of another neuron. The number of synapses per neuron varies from a few hundred to a few thousand. The strength or efficacy of signal transmission varies from synapse to synapse. The strength of the signal finally received by a cell thus depends upon both the strength of the signal coming down the axon, and upon the efficacy of synaptic transmission. Synaptic efficacies are determined by the past history of activity within the net, and, as we shall see, they play a crucial role in learning and memory.

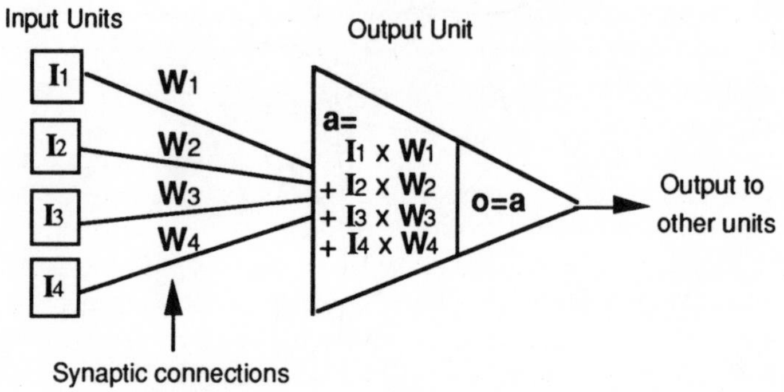

Figure 3.2. A sketch of the elementary components of simple neural net simulations. I_1 to I_4 are the units which provide input to the output unit. W_1 to W_4 are the weights on connections between each input unit and the output unit. The activation of the output unit (a) is determined using an activation function which, in this example, sums the product of each input multiplied by the weight at its connection with the output unit. The output of the unit (o) is calculated using an output function, which in this example equates activation and output.

We will call the elementary components of neural computers, units. The total input to each unit determines its state of activation, a. Exactly how this is computed from the inputs is specified by the activation function. The signal that each unit transmits to other units is its output, o, and exactly how this is computed from the activation is specified by the output function. The strength of each synaptic connection is specified by the synaptic weight. Figure 3.2 shows the elementary components diagrammatically, together with examples of commonly used activation and output functions.

In some systems the output values are constrained so that they vary between 0 and 1, and in others so that they vary between +1 and -1. In some systems the outputs take only one of two discrete values, usually either 0 or 1 or +1 or -1. In others output can vary continuously within the specified range.

Systems that allow negative output values are prima facie very different from all biological systems. When neural cells are strongly inhibited they send no signals to other cells, not negative signals. This is much more than a notational difference because it means that cells do not know how strongly other cells are inhibited beyond a certain limit, and because when a cell is silent the weights on its connections to other cells are irrelevant. With negative outputs this is not so, the weights from a cell are as relevant when it is inhibited as when it is excited.

Architectures

An enormous variety of interconnection architectures exist within biological nervous systems. In current neural computers there is much less variation. Two architectures are particularly common: auto-associative nets, and pattern-matching nets, shown in Figures 3.3 and 3.4. Most of the programs in this guide use one or other of these two architectures, but others will be introduced in Chapters 8 and 9.

Auto-associative nets can be thought of as representing the particular objects or items that the system knows about, and pattern-matching nets can be thought of as representing the associations between them. An auto-associative net is one in which each unit in the net is connected to all or many of the other units. It is called an auto-associative net because it associates parts of an input with other parts of the same input. In auto-associative nets a unit's output can change its own input. This is because units to which it sends signals may send signals back to it, which may then change its own state of activity. Rich sequences of dynamic change can therefore be generated by nets with such feed-back. One cycle of interaction in such a dynamic sequence is called an iteration. The process as a whole is called relaxation because it allows the activities of all the units to change so that they become as compatible as possible with the weights.

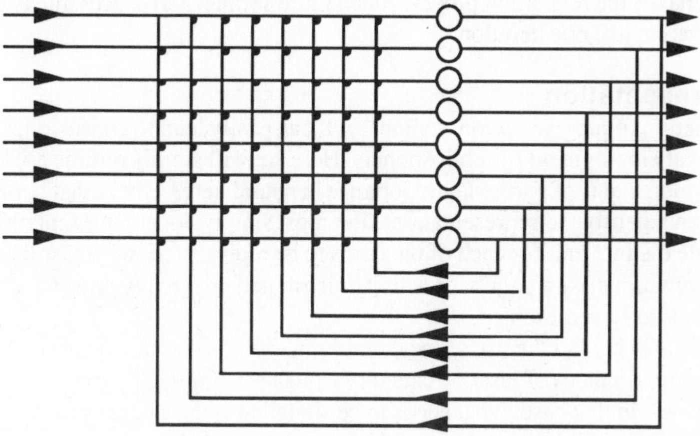

Figure 3.3. An auto-associative architecture

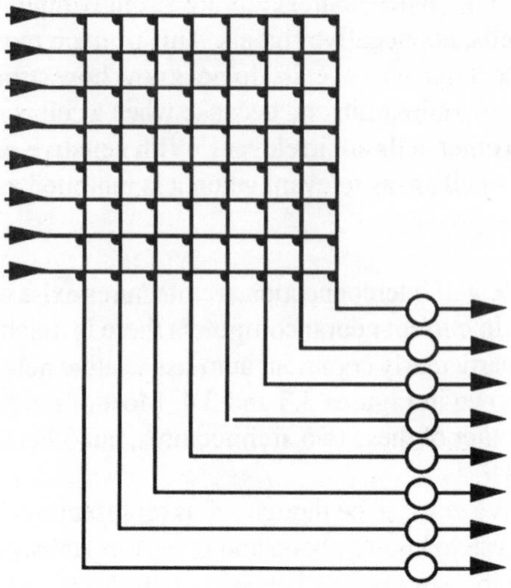

Figure 3.4. A pattern-matching architecture

A pattern-matching net is one in which units in one layer are connected to units in a succeeding layer, but do not have inter-connections within layers. They are also called layered feed-forward nets, because information is transmitted sequentially in just one direction through the layers. Such nets are typically used to associate sets of input-output pairs, so that given one of the input patterns it generates the appropriate output pattern. The absence of feed-back makes the relaxation process much more simple, and processing is usually achieved in just one iteration.

Representation

The notion of representation is slippery. It can easily lead to confusion, and so to useful employment for philosophers. Here we will simply outline a distinction that is of particular importance in neural net research: that between local and distributed representations. Put most simply, local representations use a single distinct unit for each of the items to be represented, whereas distributed representations use a pattern of activity distributed over many units for each of the items to be represented.

The idea behind the use of local representations is that in many task domains things are instances of just one category from a set of mutually exclusive categories. In that case, what needs to be signalled is the category membership of any instance. For example, the 26 letters of the alphabet are a set of mutually exclusive categories. Any instance of a letter is one and only one of these 26; which category that is can be signalled simply and directly by selecting just one unit from a set of 26 units.

The idea behind distributed representations is that things have an internal structure that is critical for many tasks. Internal structure cannot be transmitted by the activity of a single unit so it is done by using a set of units, with larger sets conveying information about richer structures. The most simple realisation of such a scheme is where items can be represented by specifying their features, and these distinct features are represented by distinct units or subsets of units. Items are then represented by the set of units that represent their features. For example, letters could be represented by a set of units where each unit stands for some feature of the letter. If different letters have some features in common then their representations will have some units in common.

Distributed representations thus differ from local ones in two ways that have fundamental computational consequences: 1) they can explicitly convey information about internal structure: 2) the similarity of two representations reflects the similarity between the things that they represent. In the simple realisation of a distributed representation just outlined local codes were used for the features (which may also be referred to as micro-features). For a more thoroughly distributed scheme the features could also be represented in a distributed way.

The choice of representational scheme has important consequences. Consider a net with N units. With a local scheme there are codes for N distinct items, and *any combination of these N items can be signalled at a time.* With a distributed scheme there are codes for N^2 different items (i.e. very many more than with a local scheme), but *only one of these can be signalled at a time*

Intermediate forms of representation are of course possible. A fully distributed scheme uses the pattern of activation across the whole set of units to represent items. A partially distributed scheme would use patterns of activation across only a sub-set of units. How local or distributed the representation is will then depend upon how large a proportion of the whole that sub-set is. The possibility of intermediate forms does not at all imply that the distinction is unimportant. The properties of the different schemes are so different that we should expect the degree to which representations are local or distributed to depend heavily upon the function to be performed.

Sensory systems must be able to present a very large number of distinct entities at any one time, and possibly any combination of all the distinct things for which they have codes. This indicates that sensory representation should be mainly local. This inference is supported by the precision of the topographic mapping that exists between the various sensory feature maps.

Within the cognitive systems that deal with concepts, however, the situation is very different. The great difference between the very large number of concepts that humans acquire and the very small number that they can have actively in mind at any one time is evidence that the representation of concepts is mainly distributed.

Processing

In real life time is often of vital importance, but nature has never discovered ways of communicating between nerve cells in less than about a millisecond. Furthermore, the effectiveness of any course of action will usually improve as more information is taken into account. Nervous systems must therefore often process a lot of information quickly despite the slowness of their elements. So they do many things at once, letting them interact as well as time allows. The result is a style of processing that emphasises functional specialisations, with dedicated machinery for specific functions. The processes of coordination within and between the specialised sub-systems are then holistic and approximate, rather than piecewise and precise.

Processing consists of changes in the state of activity of the units under the influence of external inputs and the interactions between the units. In the case of a simple auto-associative net this processing can be thought of as transforming a presented pattern of activity so as to recognise or recreate known items. What the transformation does is to create a pattern of activity that is compatible with the weights. Only a very small proportion of all possible states will be compatible with the weights. Many different initial states will therefore be transformed into one of these "attractor" states. The trick is then to use a learning rule that turns the states it needs to remember into attractors. The "retrieval of items from memory" then becomes the recreation of these learned states.

In the case of a simple pattern-matching net processing can be thought of as associating items of one kind with items of another kind. Processing in this case consists of producing a pattern of activity in one set of units given activity in another, quite distinct, set of units.

It is important to distinguish between the effects of local and global variables on processing. Local variables are specified for each unit separately. For example, the current level of activation of each unit, and the inputs being received at each of its particular synaptic connections are local variables. Different levels of activation may even be specified for different parts of each cell. As neural nets can do a lot using only local variables it is often supposed that no others are needed. However, in biological systems there are also global variables whose values are signalled widely throughout the brain. The most obvious involve the systems for arousal and alertness, but there are also others.

Learning

What a net does is determined by the interactions between its component units, and this is determined by the strengths of the connections between them. The most straightforward way to change what the net does is therefore to change the strengths of the connections, i.e. the synaptic weights. As there are approximately 10^{14} synaptic connections in the human brain. they provide ample capacity to store the information acquired during a lifetime. Modifiable synapses have long been the most plausible candidate for the biological basis of learning, and there is now a wealth of physiological and biochemical evidence that this is so.

Given that learning involves changing connection strengths, the question that arises is "What determines how they are changed?". The biological evidence shows that the main determinants of the changes to be made are the activities of the two cells connected by the synapse. A great advantage of this is that it makes learning predominantly dependent upon local variables that are specified near to the place where the change must be made. It also means that learning is activity dependent. What is learned depends upon both what inputs are received from the environment, and upon the way that the net treats them.

Simulations with this guide will enable you to explore this approach to learning. The wide extent of its adaptive radiation throughout the animal kingdom suggests that it has computational consequences of considerable value.

Perspectives on neural net research

The study of neural computation has aroused the interest and efforts of people from an unusually wide range of disciplines. Most centrally these are neurobiology, computer science, and cognitive psychology, but physicists, mathematicians, and engineers are also involved. These workers do share common goals, but their perspectives differ, and each discipline also has its own distinctive goals.

The computational perspective

The study of neural computation is concerned with the principles of computation in neural systems in general. It aims to provide a formal account of neural computation that will give us a better idea of what the computational abilities of such systems are, as well a better idea of how they can be achieved. The computational perspective contrasts two quite different kinds of computation: von Neumann computation, and neural computation. From its beginning the computer industry has focussed on a design proposed by the mathematician John von Neumann. The success of that industry demonstrates the power of the von Neumann design. Nevertheless many of the things that the human brain can do easily and naturally have turned out to be exceedingly difficult for von Neumann computers. This includes such basic and necessary things as understanding what we see, exploring our environment, and learning language. These achievements therefore demonstrate the power of the neural approach to computation. It seems to have its limitations, however, because no biological system can perform logical calculations with anything like the speed and accuracy of von Neumann computers. Thus, what they are good at we are bad at, and vice versa. This suggests that they represent quite different approaches to computation.

In the early days computers were commonly thought of as the mechanisation of the human thought processes. Just as machines were developed to help us with our physical labours, so computers would help us with our mental labours. This they have done, but the tasks for which they have been designed are the abstract intellectual tasks that we find most difficult (and which are barely possible at all for other animals). Thus abstract logical thought has been mechanised, but not the concrete intuitive cognition so characteristic of humans and other animals.

The differences between computers and brains were clear to von Neumann, and we recommend his clear little book on the subject (von Neumann, 1958). Underlying the obvious difference in their physical design is a more fundamental one. They solve different problems. In simple terms von Neumann computers are *serial symbol processors*. They manipulate symbolic expressions with great speed, precision, and reliability according to explicit and detailed instructions. Instructions and the data on which they operate are stored in memory locations specified by addresses. Operations are carried out by copying data from the memory into a central processing unit.

Neural nets compute in a wholly different way, and have been described as *parallel distributed processors*. They do not process symbols serially at great speed but transform and associate distributed patterns of activity using massive parallelism. It is inappropriate to think of these distributed patterns of activity as symbols because their internal structures are not arbitrary but dependent on their meaning. The dynamics of the system is determined more by holistic integration than by step-by-step precision.

Memory and processing are not at all distinguished as in conventional computers. Processing is determined by the connections. For computer scientists these may be thought of as the instruction set, except that there can be an enormous number of them, they are highly specialised, and they change with experience. Memories are thus stored in this instruction set. They may be thought of as remembering what to do. They do not have to be "retrieved" from a separate memory store, and copied into the processor. They are already there. Memory addressing, which is so fundamental a part of conventional computing, is wholly irrelevant.

Lastly, neural nets are not programmed, they learn. What they learn bears little resemblance to the explicit symbolic algorithms that programmers provide for conventional computers.

This sketch of the style of neural computing should not mislead the reader into supposing that the fundamental computational principles underlying neural computation are already as clear as those underlying conventional computing. They are not. Neural computing is too young for that, and still has far to go. In addition to its formal abstract goals the computational perspective includes other goals - those of engineering. There is a common assumption that theoretical abstraction and practical application are in opposition. They are not. An understanding of basic principles shows how problems might be solved. Doing it shows whether the principles and problems are understood or not.

Consider flight. Birds first showed us that it is possible. It was also obvious that their wings had something to do with it, but far from obvious what. Part of the problem was that birds' wings solve two distinct problems - propulsion and lift. The development of aeroplanes depended upon a better understanding of the problems to be solved, and upon the discovery of the underlying aerodynamic principles by which the shape of the wing provides lift.

Similarly, the attempt to understand how higher animals' cognitive achievements work faced the difficulty that nothing that we already understood worked in anything like the same way as brains. Analogies that have been used include, hydraulic systems, telephone exchanges, and serial digital computers. None of these analogies have been at all helpful, however. It is not that the appropriate analogy was there, and people simply failed to notice it. There was no relevant analogy.

The study of neural computation is based on the idea that the structure of brains may be a better guide to how they achieve what they do than the use of analogies to other systems with quite different structures and abilities. The hope that now inspires many is that by designing, testing, and improving neural computers we are developing systems that can be understood, and that work in basically the same way as brains. Initially some essential aspects of brain structure will be omitted, and some irrelevant aspects will be included, but the research strategy hopes to discover and correct these errors. This strategy is thus equivalent to that of studying simplified wing-like structures in order to find out how they help birds fly.

It is of course true that aeroplanes use a means of propulsion that is completely different from that used by birds. What matters from the engineering point of view is that things do what is required of them, not that they do so in a biological way. Nevertheless, biological solutions can both help show what the problems are and show possible strategies by which they may be solved. This guidance may be highly valuable, particularly when we otherwise have little or no idea as to how something can be done.

The biological perspective

The use of computer simulations and formal analyses of idealised neural nets to further our understanding of how real brains work is called computational neuroscience . An excellent introduction to its methods and philosophy is given by Sejnowski, Koch and Churchland (1988). The great strength of classical neuroscience has been the wealth of knowledge that it has acquired on the anatomy and physiology of nervous systems. Its great weakness has been the absence of any comparable understanding of the computational role of those structures and processes. The use of principles derived from the study of neural computation to interpret what is known about real nervous systems provides specific predictions that neurobiologists can test. The results of such tests successively refine our understanding of both the neurobiological data and the computational principles.

Real nervous systems have of course developed over enormous periods of time by haphazard evolutionary tinkering with preexisting designs in a wide variety of ecological niches. As a consequence they show enormous diversity. Our working assumption is that this great adaptive radiation of nervous systems is evidence for the existence of general and powerful principles of neural computation, not evidence against them.

We do not suppose that just one set of computational principles are embodied in all regions of all nervous systems. The evidence suggests that this is not the case. There may be some principles common to all neural systems, but there are also likely to be principles that apply only to some.

From a cognitive point of view the neural systems of greatest relevance, are those of the mammalian cortex and its closely linked thalamic systems. The evidence from neurobiology (e.g., Mountcastle, 1978) and neuropsychology (e.g., Luria, 1973) clearly indicates that the overall organisation of the cortex is modular. It has been estimated that there are between 100 and 200 functionally distinct regions in each human cortical hemisphere. Different regions represent information about different kinds of things. For example, some may be specialised to enable us to say words, others to enable us to recognise them when we see them, and yet others to associate them with various aspects of their meanings.

There must be some similarities in the way that the different regions work simply by virtue of their all being devices that compute with neurons. In addition, however, there is evidence for a specifically cortical mode of organisation. The simple idea is that, although *what* the modules represent differs, *how* they do it and how they learn to do so is common to all. This view is summarised by what Wolf Singer, Director of Neurophysiology in the Max Planck Institute for Brain Research in Frankfurt, calls his credo: "The cortical algorithm is everywhere the same".

The anatomical and physiological evidence for the existence of a common cortical algorithm is extensive (e.g., Mountcastle, 1978). There are variations in anatomy across the neo-cortex, and on the basis of these differences Brodmann identified about 50 different areas per human hemisphere. Many of these differences are so subtle, however, that anatomists often deny their existence. Even across widely different species cortical structure remains remarkably constant. The area and thickness of the cortex varies greatly, but its internal structure does not. The columnar and hyper-columnar organisation, first discovered in somatic and visual primary areas, also appears to be repeated in all the areas whose functional organisation is known (Mountcastle, 1978). The neuroanatomists, Rockel, Hiorns, and Powell (1980), in an article titled "The basic uniformity in structure of the neo-cortex", say "The significance of the columnar organisation is in the processing of incoming information, vertically within a column, and horizontally between columns, with a wide and diverse distribution of the results through the pyramidal cell axons; the form of the processing might be essentially similar in all areas but the differences in function between areas would be due to the differences in the sources and termination of their connections" p239.

In summary, evolution obviously discovered systems with enormous computational potential in neural nets. It is now feasible to search for the design principles on which these systems are based. Some principles apply to neural systems in general, others only to particular systems. Special computational abilities seem to arise in the mammalian cortico-thalamic system by the repeated application of a powerful general purpose procedure - the cortical algorithm. A major goal is to discover exactly what the these abilities are and how they arise from the cortical architecture.

The psychological perspective

The central goal of cognitive psychology is to understand human cognition. Perception, learning, language and thought are the basic processes with which it is concerned. Verbal thought plays such a large role in our conscious experience, that it is very easy to suppose that intelligence and cognition in general are much the same as conscious verbal thought. This assumption is often seen in analogies between minds and von Neumann computers, which as we argued earlier can be seen as a further development of the serial symbol processing computational style of verbal thought.

One problem facing any review of the serial symbol processing analogy is that it is so deeply embedded within our thinking that it is difficult to adopt ways of thinking about cognition that are radically different. Conceptions of parallel distributed processing may provide an alternative framework, particularly as developed by Rumelhart and McClelland (1986) and their many colleagues. Central to this development has been the belief that PDP systems naturally display many of the basic abilities of human cognition, such as context sensitivity, the ability to deal with fuzzy information, access to memories through their content rather than their address, effective generalisation of knowledge to new situations, rule-like behaviour without access to explicit rules, fault tolerance, and so on.

The psychological perspective therefore focuses on the attempt to explain these and other human cognitive abilities in terms of the computations that neural systems can actually carry out. Our simulations and the exercises in this manual try to introduce you to ways in which this might be possible.

Suggestions for further reading

Introductions to neural computing are given in the primary source references (p.113). For an introduction to both the biological bases and the philosophical implications see Churchland (1986). A succinct outline of the nature and aims of computational neuroscience is provided by Sejnowski et al (1988).

4

Lateral Inhibition

This module has three aims:

1) to show how neural nets with lateral inhibition emphasise differences between neighbouring inputs.
2) to familiarise the user with the conventions and operating procedures that are used throughout this package.
3) to show the steps that are involved in calculating the activation and output of units in a net.

Lateral inhibition is a very common pattern of connectivity in biological nervous systems. Its essential feature is the inhibition of neurons to the side of, or around, the activated neurons. Its two main forms are feed-forward and recurrent. Feed-forward is the simplest. Nets with feed-forward lateral inhibition have two layers of cells. Each cell in the first layer excites the cell in the corresponding position in the second layer and inhibits the neighbours of that cell. In the recurrent form there is reciprocal lateral inhibition between cells in the same layer. In this case cells can inhibit the cells that are trying to inhibit them, and can thus affect their own input. They can also indirectly affect the activity of cells further away than their nearest neighbours. These secondary consequences arise because the inhibition applies to the cells doing the inhibiting. They mean that the final state of activation of the net is not determined in just one step. In the feed-forward case neither of these secondary consequences apply and the output can be calculated from the input in just one step.

Program One: Perceptual phenomena related to lateral inhibition

Three visual illusions due to lateral inhibition are: 1) simultaneous brightness contrast; 2) the Chevreul illusion, and; 3) Mach bands. Ernst Mach, the German physicist and philosopher, proposed an explanation of such psychological phenomena in terms of lateral inhibition in 1865, long before there was any direct physiological or anatomical evidence for it. This is therefore a very early demonstration that psychological observations can provide valuable insights into the design and operation of neural networks. Mach and Helmholtz helped begin the psychophysical research tradition that relates psychology to both the physics of stimulation and the physiology of the nervous system. This research strategy has since been especially well developed and fruitful in the domain of visual psychophysics.

To see these perceptual phenomena select Program One on the Lateral Inhibition menu, and click *Continue* to move through the demonstrations. The Mach band illusions are less obvious than the other two but may become clearer if you look steadily at the centre of the display.

We have so far discussed network structure, and some consequent illusions. In addition we must also ask "Why is lateral inhibition so common in nervous systems? What is its function?". Put simply, its role is to accentuate differences. In vision it picks out the boundaries between brighter and darker areas. This is useful because such boundaries often signal the edges of objects, or important markings on their surfaces. In more general terms, it increases responses to the regions of the input where there are differences, and decreases responses to regions where the input is homogeneous. This is valuable because much important information is contained in the relative values that is not contained in the absolute values considered independently.

Program Two: Feed-forward lateral inhibition

This module illustrates two important aspects of neural nets that you must learn to distinguish: 1) the architecture of the neural network; and 2) the processes carried out within that architecture.

Architecture

The units of our simulated nets are idealised abstractions of nerve cells as described in Chapter 3. At the simplest level of network architecture a small number of units are connected in a particular way to form a micro-circuit. Figure 4.1. shows the micro-circuit used in this simulation. It has 4 units: 1 in the first layer, and 3 in the second. The unit in the first layer receives input from outside the net, e.g. it may be a visual receptor specialised to transduce light quanta to electro-chemical signals. It has excitatory connections to the central unit in the second layer, and inhibitory connections to its two lateral neighbours.

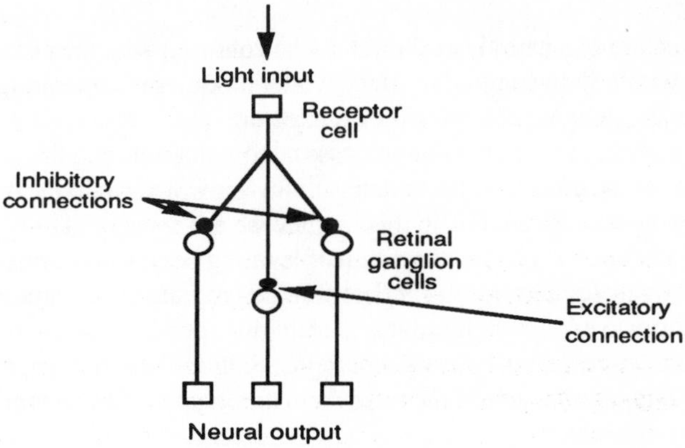

Figure 4.1. A feed-forward lateral inhibitory micro-circuit

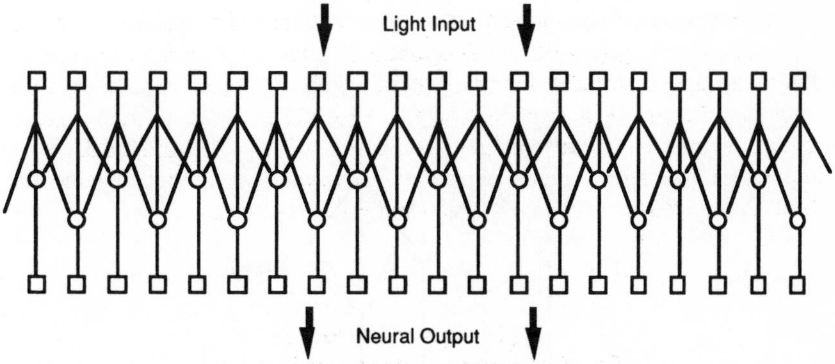

Figure 4.2. A lateral feed-forward inhibitory net

This simple micro-circuit can be used to build a net with very many more units by joining lots of them together. Figure 4.2. shows how this can be done to form a one-dimensional array. In this simulation the architecture has 2 layers each of 20 units, which is formed by simply replicating the micro-circuit of Figure 4.1. This basic design can be extended to cover two or more dimensions, and the results are much the same as in the simpler one dimensional case studied here.

A great deal of the vast structural complexity of higher nervous systems comes from the replication of very much simpler micro-circuits over and over again. This is important because it supports the hope that simple principles can explain much of the apparent complexity that appears in the neural anatomy.

Processes

The architecture of a neural net should not be confused with the processes occurring within it. In some of the nets in later modules the operating processes can be changed without changing the architecture.

There are two main classes of processes: those determining the activation and outputs of the units; and those determining growth and decline of the synaptic connection strengths. In this module we are concerned only with activation and output. The investigation of learning begins in the next chapter.

Here the rule (or algorithm) for determining the state of activation of the units is simply to add up their inputs. Thus in this specific case the rule is:

The activation of each unit is equal to the input to the unit from its corresponding receptor minus the input from the receptors' two nearest lateral neighbours.

The input to the unit from its own receptor is equal to the input intensity to the receptor multiplied by the excitatory value at the connection. The inhibitory input to the unit is equal to the input intensity to the two lateral receptors multiplied by the strength of the inhibition.

In the diagram below, excitation is set at 1 and inhibition at 0.2.

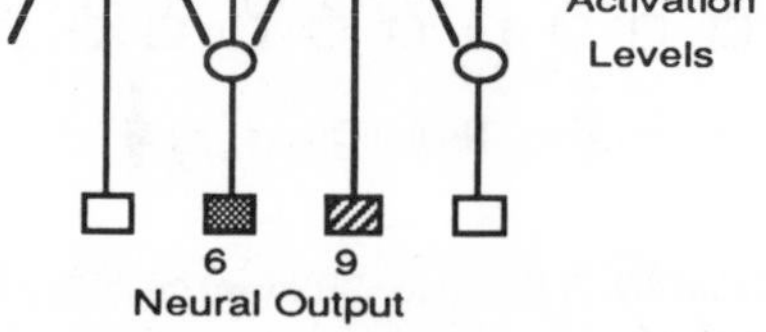

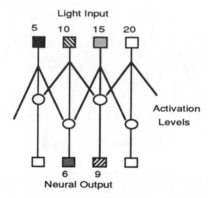

Figure 4.3. Calculating total activation.
The neural activation of 6 is calculated by Input (10) x Excitation (1) minus Input (5) x Inhibition(0.2) + Input (15) x Inhibition (0.2)i.e.: Activation =10 - (1 + 3) = 6

In Figure 4.3 the rule for determining the output of the units is just the same as the activation. i.e output = activation. In other cases less simple functions relating output to activation are used, but most are easy to understand.

How to use the program

Select *Lateral inhibition* from the main menu. A new menu for Lateral inhibition will be presented. Select *Feed-forward Lateral inhibition.* Step through the introduction by clicking *Continue.*

After a simple outline of how the net works you will be presented with an 18 unit net. Light input values and neural output values are shown in squares. Activation levels (if above zero) are shown by open circles that fill as they become activated. Excitatory and inhibitory connections are shown by filled circles. The sizes of the circles show the strengths of the connections.

Items in the control panel at the top of the screen can be selected by positioning the pointer and clicking the mouse button. Their use is as follows:
Excite: This enables you to specify the strength of the excitatory connections between the units and their corresponding receptor cells. To change the value, click on "*Excite*" and a scale (0 to 1) will appear underneath. Point to the chosen value and click again.
Inhibition: This enables you to specify the strength of the inhibitory connections. The procedure is the same as for *Excite*.
Threshold: Units can be given an activation threshold value which has to be exceeded before the units will transmit an output. Initially there is no threshold, i.e. output equals activation. A threshold may be specified using the same procedure as for the previous two parameters.
Input: The light intensity pattern across all units is initially set to represent a white band on a grey background. To change this select *Input*. Move the pointer to embrace the receptor units. Select a chosen unit and then select the value for that unit from the scale (0 to 20) that will appear over it. When you have finished modifying the input [review instructions for selecting items in Chapter 2] return to the control panel.
Show graph: Graphs of the current inputs and outputs can be shown by clicking this. These will be added to any existing graphs, so that comparisons between earlier and current outputs can be made.
Clear graph: This clears all currently displayed graphs so that a clean start can be made.
Options: This provides access to further control options. In this case they are *Quit*, *Restart Program*, and *Clear Threshold*. The latter can be used to change a threshold of 0 (i.e. transmit only positive values), to the default of no threshold.

Exercises

Here we suggest some useful exercises, but you should also explore the system for yourself.

Calculating activation and output

First note that the default value for excitation and inhibition is 0, and that there is no output threshold. With these values the neural output is zero. Set the value of the excitation parameter to 1, and note how the dots showing the size of the excitatory weights increase in size.

The activation function. The activations of the units are shown by the extent to which the open circular units are filled. Their outputs are shown by the filling of the squares, and also by the numbers beneath the squares. Click *Clear graph* then *Show graph* to see a graph of the output. In the simplest possible case where *Excite* = 1, *Inhibit* = 0, and there is no output threshold, the neural output from the net equals the light input. Now add some inhibition. Set *Excite* to 1 and *Inhibit* to 0.1. Click *Show graph* to see a graph of the output. Repeat with a few other values for these two parameters. To be sure that you understand what is going on work out for yourself what the outputs should be, and compare what you get with the values shown.

The output function. With no output threshold the output of each unit is identical to its activation. This allows the output to become negative when the inhibitory input exceeds the excitatory input. This is a disadvantage because real neurons do not produce negative outputs. A simple modification of the output function is therefore to transmit only the positive values. This can be done by setting the threshold parameter to 0. Do this and explore its effects.

Graphs of these two simple output functions are shown in Figure 4.5. You can at any time switch back and forth between having and not having an output threshold by using *Threshold* to set one, and *Clear Threshold* (which is found under *Options*) to remove it.

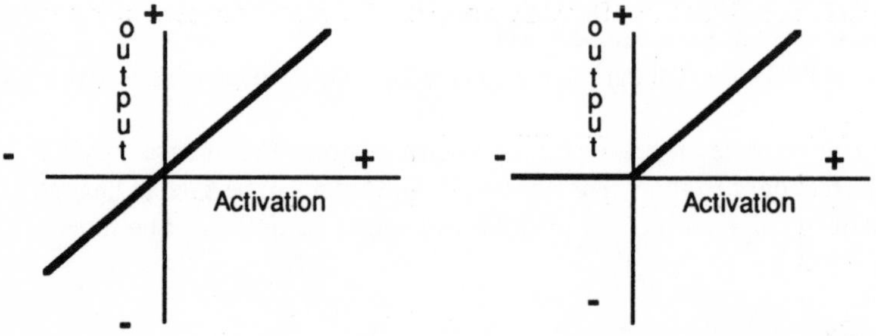

output = activation

if activation > 0 output = activation
if activation < 0 output = 0

Figure 4.4. Two simple output functions.

Edge detection

Regions where the input intensity changes sharply often signal objects' edges, so lateral inhibition in early visual processing helps in the detection of edges.

Your task in this exercise is to set the parameters to produce a simulation of edge enhancement. The outcome required is one in which neural output is greater where input intensity is changing than where it is not.

Questions: What happens when the default input distribution is used with parameter settings of Excite= 1, Inhibit= 0.3, and Threshold = 9? What important information is missing from the output in this case? Do these parameter settings give the same kind of outcome for all size steps in input intensity?

Removing responses to steady states

Consider a silhouette drawing:

Little help in understanding the picture comes from the steady state black and white areas. All the important information is contained in the boundary where there are changes in light intensity. A lateral inhibitory net can be designed so that it responds only to changes, and does not respond at all to homogeneous inputs.

It is possible to set the parameters of our net so that neural output is produced only where input intensity is changing, and which work for any size of change. In this exercise your task is to set the excitatory and inhibitory parameters to produce this effect. One possible outcome is shown in Figure 4.5.

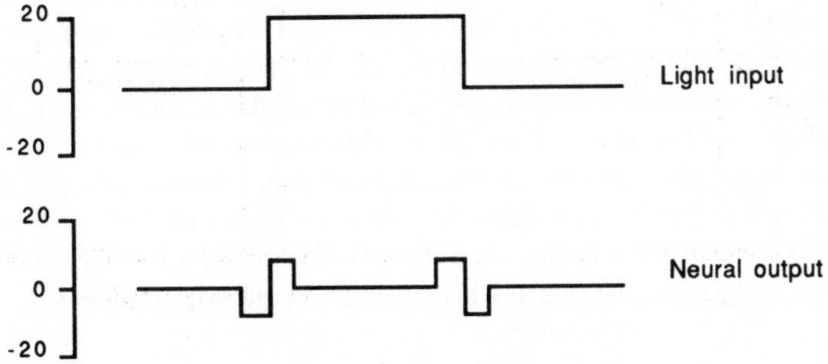

Figure 4.5. Removal of responses to steady-states

Questions: Various combinations of the excitatory and inhibitory values will give the required result. All have the same relationship between excitation and inhibition. What is it? Can the required result be achieved using only positive outputs, i.e. with Threshold = 0? You may notice that the peaks in the output signal the position of the bright side of the intensity boundary. Can the parameters of this simple system be set so that output peaks signal the position of the dark side of the boundary?

Responses to spots of light

It is very common for neurophysiologists to shine a small spot of light onto the retina, and to study how the activity of a visual cell that they are recording from changes its activity as they move the spot about. Typically they plot the areas of input stimulation that produce increases in firing rate, and also those that produce decreases in firing rate. These areas together show what is called the receptive field of the cell. This exercise provides a simple analogy to this procedure.

Click *Input,* set one input to 20, and all the other background inputs to 0. Remove any output threshold that you have set. Set *Excite* = 0.8 and *Inhibit* = 0.4. The activity across the set of output units then shows the receptive fields of our units. That is, in this net each cell is excited by light at the centre of its field, and inhibited by light in its surround.

Repeat except with all the background inputs set to 10 rather than to 0.

Responses to ramps

Ramps are regions where there is a gradual linear incline from one steady level of input to another higher level. These are the input patterns that produce the Mach Band illusion. One ramp-like stimulus that you could use is 0, 0, 0, 5, 10, 15, 20, 20 20.

With *Excite* set at 0.8 and *Inhibit* at 0.2 an "illusory" dip in output is seen at the beginning of the ramp, and an "illusory" peak is seen at the top of the ramp. These effects resemble those experienced by subjects looking at such displays, and they are also similar to distributions seen in physiological recordings of the outputs from simple retinas. Note also that this net reduces the rate at which neural output increases as input intensity increases. This will be useful in vision because light intensities in the real world vary by factors of many thousands.

With the parameters set so that steady state inputs produce no output (e.g. *Excite* = 0.8 and *Inhibit* = 0.4), the net produces output only where there ramp begins and ends. (For the mathematically minded this illustrates the fact that the output of this particular net reflects the second derivative of input intensity with respect to position. That is, this net does not compute the rate at which the input intensity changes, but the rate at which changes in intensity change.)

Program Three: Recurrent lateral inhibition

In the feed-forward net of Program Two the inhibition is produced by the units providing the input to the net. Here it is produced by the units providing the output from the net. We saw in Program Two that adding inhibition changes the output; the same thing happens here, but with the important difference that the change in output can then change the inhibition that is produced. That is, the inhibition changes the output, which changes the inhibition, and so. The output from the net can therefore change over time, even when the input to the net is constant.

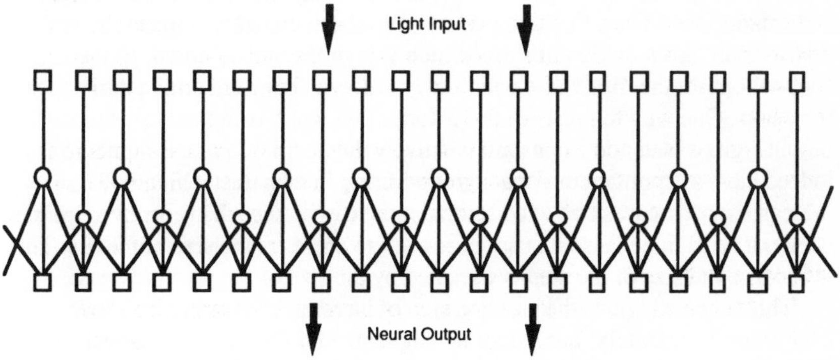

Figure 4.6. A recurrent lateral inhibition net

How to use the program

The program is used in just the same way as Program Two except that here you can cycle activity around the net to see the changes over time. Click *Cycle* to run one more cycle of activity through the net. Click *Options* and then *Restart Cycle* to restart the cycles from the beginning. Click *Restart Cycle* then *Clear Mess* if the graphs have become too large and have overflowed onto the net display.

Exercises

All the exercises suggested for the feed-forward net can be repeated with this recurrent net. Here however you should also explore the change in output over time as the interactions are cycled within the net.

Questions: Does output change over time when Inhibition = 0? What is the effect of the amount of inhibition on the number of cycles that it takes for the net to settle down to giving a steady output? Can both edge enhancement and the removal of steady state processing be achieved with this net? Repeat the single light spot experiment suggested for Program Two, first with no output threshold, then with Threshold = 0. Why do the observed effects occur?

Discussion

The output pattern shown in Figure 4.5 involves negative outputs, these can be removed by setting the output threshold to 0. Doing this removes important information, however. Positive peaks show where there are steps in the input distribution, but they do not show which side of the step is down. In the original output the dips show which way is down. They are on the dark sides of the peaks. One way to preserve this information while using only positive output signals is to add a constant positive value to all outputs. Real neurons do indeed have a "spontaneous" background firing rate against which both increases or decreases due to additional input can be seen. This background rate need not be high because it is not necessary to preserve the size of the dip. This is because the size of the step is signalled by the size of the positive peak.

This scheme signals the size and sign of increments in intensity above background accurately, but it does not signal the size of decrements well. To signal the size of large dips in the input mammalian visual systems use a further refinement: lateral excitation with central inhibition, i.e. cells that are just the opposite of the output cells in our simple net. These respond to small spots of darkness in the same way that the cells with lateral inhibition and central excitation respond to small spots of light. They are called off-centre cells, in contrast to those of our net, which are called on-centre cells.

The neural micro-circuitry underlying lateral inhibition in human vision is not as simple as that used in this program, but the processes are similar and the effects are much the same. One difference is that in all mammalian visual systems the inhibition is mediated by inhibitory inter-neurons rather than being produced directly by collaterals of the axons that also produce the excitatory throughput. The receptor cells in this module produce inhibition at some terminals and excitation at others. Biological neurons rarely do this. They either produce excitation at all of their terminals or inhibition at all of their terminals. We know of no computational advantages to the greater network complexity that this entails.

Explanations of psychological perceptual phenomena in terms of lateral inhibition assume that the brightness distributions of which we are consciously aware are directly related to the distributions of neural output. This implies that each point of which we are conscious corresponds to the output of a single cell. Is this plausible? How could it ever be tested?

This important issue is unresolved. Some think that there is evidence that elements of consciousness can correspond to the activity of single cells. Others think that elements of consciousness always correspond to the activity of cellular populations.

This raises the issue of the functions of consciousness. These may be best understood by showing what neural systems can compute with consciousness that they cannot compute without it. We know of no clear and convincing account of this sort.

In the general introduction to this chapter we said that the usual function proposed for lateral inhibition is to detect regions of the input where there are contrasts. This is O.K. as far as sensory processing is concerned, but lateral inhibition occurs very generally throughout nervous systems, and not just in areas concerned with sensory processing. This suggests that we should keep in mind that there may be a more general way of describing its function. This may have to do with the need to preserve small differences between sets of values when they are transmitted through noisy channels with a low dynamic range, i.e. through channels that cannot preserve a wide range of absolute values accurately.

Suggestions for further reading

For an elementary and well-illustrated introduction to neural information processing and lateral inhibition in the context of cognition see Lindsay and Norman (1972), Chapter 2. For a thorough but lucid presentation of all the basic facts and arguments see Cornsweet (1970). The two classic books devoted entirely to lateral inhibition are *Mach Bands: Quantitative studies on neural networks in the retina*, Ratliff (1965); and *Sensory inhibition*, von Bekesy (1967). For a computational analysis of human vision that is especially coherent and insightful see Watt (1988). Phillips and Singer (1974) and Singer and Phillips (1974) present an account of the detection of temporal contrasts that was tested both by using neurophysiology to make psychological predictions, and by using psychology to make physiological predictions. Finally, for an advanced review of the neurophysiological foundations of visual perception see Spillmann and Werner (1990).

5

Auto-Association

This module introduces some of the fundamental concepts in neural computation. The user is advised to ensure a good grasp of them before proceeding further.

The primary function of auto-associative memories is to learn, store, and reconstruct patterns. They are called auto-associative because they work by associating the various parts of a pattern with each other. The basic form of an auto-associative neural net is one layer of units in which each unit is connected at synapses to all of the other units. This architecture is shown in Figure 5.1. Each unit can be thought of as representing some part or feature of a pattern. The pattern as a whole is therefore represented by a pattern of activity across the whole set of units, and not by the activity of any single unit.

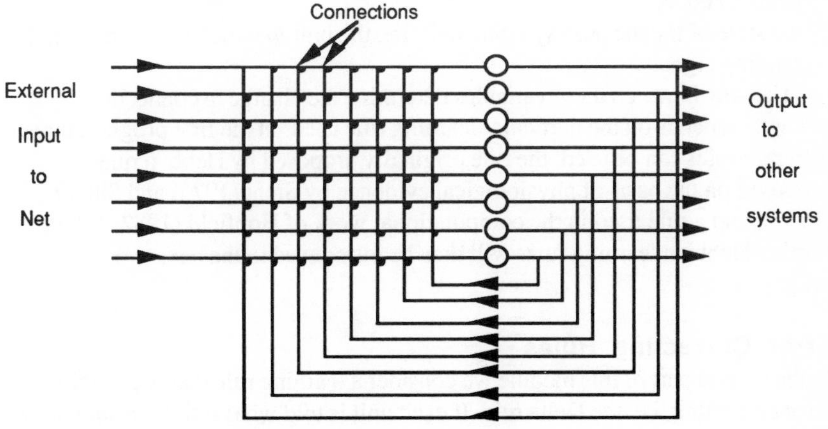

Fig 5.1. A single-layer auto-associative net

Each synaptic connection between units has a transmission value or weight as in the Lateral Inhibition module. In the auto-associative nets simulated here weights can be positive, negative, or zero, and can change between these values during learning. As each pattern is presented the weights are adjusted in a way that depends on the learning rule.

Once the net has "learned" the set of patterns it can be "tested" to see how well the patterns can be recalled. Often part of a learned pattern is presented to see whether the net can then reconstruct the whole learned pattern. The human equivalent of this is the ability to reconstruct a complete memory from a fragment or cue. Human memory is very good at doing this, but it often occurs without our noticing it.

We have already said that the weights at connections between units are adjusted as each pattern in the set is presented. The patterns (memories) are therefore stored in a configuration (matrix) of weights. Memory of the patterns is spread across many connections, and is not stored in any single location. This concept is sometimes difficult to grasp but should become clearer after using the simulations.

Rules for changing the weights, or connection strengths, can be divided into two main types:

Hebbian Rules

In the first part of this module we will introduce rules that derive from the pioneering work of Donald Hebb in the late 1940s (Hebb, 1949). They are distinguished by their use of just two main variables to determine how the connection strength should change:

1) the state of the pre-synaptic unit, i.e. the unit *from* which the connection is getting signals.
2) the state of the the post-synaptic unit, i.e. the unit *to* which the connection is sending signals.

The way in which these variables determine the change in connection strength depends on the particular learning rule used. In the first program three different rules can be used: the rule originally proposed by Hebb; a rule proposed on the basis of physiological evidence by Stent (1973) and Singer (1987); and a rule used in the computational work of Hopfield (1982, 1984). Further Hebbian learning rules will then be introduced in the next two programs.

Error Correcting Rules

In the second part of this module we consider a learning rule that is explicitly error correcting, i.e. the Delta rule. If each unit is told what activity *it should be producing* then it can compare that with the activity that *it is producing* to measure the error in its response. The weights can then be changed in a way that reduces this error.

If a pattern to be learned is presented to the net then we want it to produce

the same pattern as output. That is, we want the pattern that the net generates internally to be the same as that which it is receiving from the outside. The desired output of each unit for each input pattern is therefore determined. The activity generated by the net may differ from the desired output at any given time and the difference between these two may be regarded as an error. The weights are changed to minimise the error for each pattern. The Delta rule therefore uses three terms to adjust the weights:
1) the state of the pre-synaptic unit,
2) the state of the post-synaptic unit that is generated by the net,
3) the "desired" or "target" state of the post-synaptic unit.

Outline of the auto-associative programs

There are five programs in this module:

Introduction to Hebbian rules

The purpose of this program is to make three simple Hebbian learning rules clear, and to show that performance depends upon the relations between the different patterns learned.

Character storage in a Hebbian net

The purpose of this program is to familiarise you with the way in which you can present patterns to be learned, and to introduce you to more general forms of the Hebbian learning rules.

Build your own Hebbian net

Experienced users will find this the best program for studying Hebbian rules in an auto-associative net. The net can have up to 25 units, and can be trained with up to 14 patterns. The sizes of the increases and decreases in synaptic weight can also be specified. Exercises using this program are designed to show the basic computational capabilities of auto-associative memories.

Introduction to the Delta rule

The purpose of this program is to make the way that the Delta rule works clear.

Build your own Delta net

Experienced users will find this the best program for studying the Delta rule in an auto-associative net. The net built can have up to 25 units, and can be trained with up to 14 patterns.

Program One: Introduction to Hebbian rules

The program demonstrates an auto-associative memory with eight units mutually inter-connected at synapses. Each synaptic connection has a transmission value or weight. Weights can be positive (excitatory), negative (inhibitory), or zero. The activation level of each unit is the sum of the external input to that unit plus the weighted input from all the other units. The change in weights on the connections depends upon the learning rule applied to the net. Three learning rules can be studied. All three are called Hebbian, or Hebb-like, rules. They are shown in Figure 5.2.

Post-synaptic activity	+	+	0	0
Pre-synaptic activity	+	0	+	0
Hebb	+a			
Stent-Singer	+a	-a		
Hopfield	+a	-a	-a	+a

Figure 5.2. The Hebb, Stent-Singer, and Hopfield rules for changing weights: a is a parameter that specifies the size of the change

The Hebb Rule

Modification of the weights at connections occurs only when both pre-synaptic and post-synaptic units are active. The connection is then strengthened. Connections are not weakened. See Hebb (1949), page 62, for the original statement of this rule.

The Stent-Singer Rule

Modification of the weights occurs only when the post-synaptic unit is active. Weights at connections with active pre-synaptic units are then strengthened, and weights at connections with inactive pre-synaptic units are weakened. See Stent (1973) and Singer (1987) for physiological evidence for this rule.

The Hopfield Rule

When the pre-synaptic and post-synaptic units are in the same state (i.e. either both active or both inactive) connections are strengthened. When the pre-synaptic and post-synaptic units are in different states (i.e. one active and the other inactive) the connection is weakened. For this rule see Hopfield (1984).

How to use the program

The demonstration program is in two sections. Section One shows the performance of the net when the patterns to be stored have no common parts. Section Two shows performance when they do.

The program has only limited user interaction. The symbol system is the same as in the Lateral Inhibition module.

Once you have read six pages of screen text you will be presented with an 8-unit net with a control panel located at the top of the screen. The menu includes the three learning rules. The aim of this program is to show how the input pattern and the learning rule determine the resulting weights matrix (the distributed way of storing the input patterns).

Note: An auto-associative net is a parallel processing device, but in order to demonstrate how the weights are assigned this simulation shows the parallel process in a serial form, changing the weights from only one unit at a time.

Section One: Patterns without shared features

Select a learning rule then click *Continue* three times, and read the footnotes on the screen. Thereafter each time you click on *Learn* you will see one pathway highlighted indicating the post-synaptic and pre-synaptic inputs to connections. The pre-synaptic unit is the unit from which the synapse receives its signal. The post-synaptic unit is the unit to which the synapse sends signals. Thus since all units in this net send signals to all the others each is pre-synaptic to the other seven units. Describing a unit as pre-synaptic or post-synaptic is therefore describing it relative to a specified synapse. All units are pre-synaptic relative to some synapses, and post-synaptic relative to others.

Follow the highlighted route to determine the pre-synaptic inputs at each connection. It might help you understand the weight changes if you concentrate on one particular unit, say unit 4. The Stent-Singer rule, for example, specifies that weights at connections are only modified when the post-synaptic cell is active (i.e., the connections *to* units 1 4 5 7). It then specifies that weights on connections from active pre-synaptic units are increased, and that those from inactive units are decreased. Hence the weight changes on the connections *from* the other units to unit 4 are:

Unit 1 = 1 = increase
Unit 2 = 0 = decrease
Unit 3 = 0 = decrease
Unit 5 = 1 = increase
Unit 6 = 0 = decrease
Unit 7 = 1 = increase
Unit 8 = 0 = decrease

You should be clear on how the weights are modified before continuing.

To input Pattern B keep clicking *Continue* and then *Learn*.

When both patterns have been learned, click *Test* to present a test pattern to the net. If you make an error during pattern input, simply select and reset the erroneous bit. Exit back to the main control panel. Check *Test* 5 times and observe the cycles of interaction within the net as it responds to the test pattern.

For each test cycle the input is presented to the net. The activation for each unit is computed by adding the external (test) input to the input from every other unit. The input from the other units (the internal input) is determined by the activation of each unit multiplied by the weight. Output is then set equal to the activation.

Section Two: Patterns with shared features

To proceed from Section One to Section Two click *Options*, *Quit*, and *Continue to next program.*

The patterns used in Section One did not share any active units. In mathematical terms the two patterns were orthogonal to each other. Orthogonal pattern sets are easy to learn because the weight changes caused by each pattern do not affect the weights produced by previous patterns. Only a tiny proportion of all possible pattern sets are orthogonal, however. Furthermore, patterns in the real world usually share common features, and some of the most useful capabilities of auto-associative memories, such as abstraction, arise from the shared representation of these shared features.

Section Two therefore shows what happens when the different patterns learned share active units. This section of the program is controlled in the same way as Section One. Please check that you understand clearly why weights at connections are assigned as they are. One good way of achieving this is a predict-and-check procedure for each connection. Weights for the two patterns are summed, so that in some cases positive and negative weights will cancel to zero, while in other cases large positive or negative weights are established.

Exercises

An auto-associative net has useful capacities. For example, the net can reproduce a whole pattern given only a part (pattern completion). In computer terminology this is called a content addressable memory, because the content, or part of it, is used to find the whole memory.

Simple pattern completion

Use Section Two and the Hopfield rule. Click *Continue* until both patterns A and B are learned. Click *Test* and a scale (0-1) will be presented above the inputs. Point at input unit 1, click the button, then point at 0.1 and click again. You should see a small square inside the input box with "0.1" beside it. Repeat this for unit 2. Exit and return to menu.

Cycle 1: units 1 and 2 are activated by the external (test) input only. There is no internal input yet so no other units are activated.

Cycle 2: units 6 and 8 are now also activated because they receive excitatory internal input from units 1 and 2. The activation of units 1 and 2 also grows because they now receive excitatory internal input in addition to the external input they are receiving.

Cycles 3, 4, 5: the activation of all units associated with pattern A are mutually increased until pattern A is completed.

You can repeat this exercise for various parts of each of the two learned patterns, and using each of the three learning rules.

Capabilities and limitations of the simple Hebb rule

Use Section One of Program One, select Hebb, and click *Continue* until both patterns are learned. Note that the weight matrix is wholly excitatory. Testing will then show that each pattern can be reconstructed from any part whatsoever. This capability is marred by the fact that if a test input is presented that contains all or most of one pattern, but very little of the other, the net does not choose the pattern that is closest to the input, but simply ends up with an output that is the sum of the two learned patterns.

Next, proceed to Section Two and select Hebb. Test by presenting an element that is part of just one of the two patterns. The net does not just complete that learned pattern as in Section One but ends up in a state that is the sum of both learned patterns.

The limitations of the simple original Hebb rule arise because it does not specify any conditions under which weights should decrease. These limitations are severe. Furthermore there is neurophysiological evidence that synaptic strength can be weakened as well as strengthened. Most associative memories therefore use rules that both increase and decrease weights. It is such rules that will be examined most closely in the following programs.

Program Two: Character storage in a Hebbian net

This program gives you greater control by allowing input of your own patterns. The program also allows you to more easily compare and test the weights matrices resulting from the application of each of the learning rules. The program has been designed to facilitate study of the dependence between input patterns. You should already be aware from earlier demonstrations that the capacity of the net to recall stored patterns may decrease when units are active in more than one pattern. This can severely limit the net's usefulness.

Consider, for example, the present auto-associative net which is designed to store characters such as letters or numbers. Any character can be decomposed into constituent parts or features. If the net stores the characters as the associations between these parts then it must allow each feature to be part of a number of different characters.

Here we also extend and generalise our study of Hebbian learning rules. Figure 5.3 shows three classes of Hebbian synaptic plasticity studied by Willshaw and Dayan (1990). We call the first class of rule post-synaptic because change requires the post-synaptic cell to be active. Connections from active inputs are then increased by an amount a, and connections from inactive inputs are decreased by an amount b. The Stent-Singer rule is the special case of this rule when a and b are equal.

The second class is called pre-synaptic because the occurrence of change requires the pre-synaptic cell to be active. Connections to active cells are then increased by an amount a, and connections to inactive ones are decreased by an amount b. For physiological evidence for a rule of this sort see Stanton and Sejnowski (1989).

The third class is called covariance by Willshaw and Dayan (1990) because weights are increased when pre- and post-synaptic cells are in the same state, and are decreased when they are in different states. The Hopfield rule is the special case of this rule when a, b, c, and d are all equal.

Post-synaptic activity	+	+	0	0
Pre-synaptic activity	+	0	+	0
Post-synaptic	+a	-b		
Pre-synaptic	+a		-c	
Covariance	+a	-b	-b	+d

Figure 5.3. Three classes of Hebbian learning. The parameters a, b, c and d specify the sizes of the changes to be made

In this program we have set the a, b, c, and d parameters all equal. The Post-synaptic rule here is thus the same as the Stent-Singer rule in Program One, and the Covariance rule is the same as the Hopfield rule.

Willshaw and Dayan (1990) studied pattern matching nets, and show that in some cases optimum performance requires all four parameters to be different. In auto-associative nets optimum performance requires b and c to be equal, so that in our case there are only three parameters to specify. They also show that making the parameters all equal is optimal only when units are active about half of the time in the patterns to be learned. In Program Three you will be able to specify different values for these parameters.

How to use the program

Most of the procedures are the same as in Program One, but the use of *Learning Rules* and *Learn* are different. Here you can input up to 14 of your own patterns.

Select a learning rule, and input your patterns by clicking *Learn.*

Input active units by selecting the unit and clicking the mouse button. The input square will fill to denote an active input. If you wish to change an active input unit to inactive, point at the unit and click again. When you have completed the input pattern exit to the control panel. The weights matrix is automatically presented for the pattern and learning rule you have chosen.

The weights matrix for the other learning rules can be displayed by selecting the appropriate rule on the control panel. You do *not* need to input the patterns again for each rule. This means that once learning has taken place you can compare the weights matrices for the pattern set and test the net under each of the three rules, noting any differences in the net's performance.

Exercises

Characters not sharing features

First have the net learn two characters such as a 4 (units 3, 4, 6 and 8) and an L (units 2, 5, and 7). Then test with various parts of one of these patterns, and various combinations of them. Compare the different learning rules. Watching how the weights change as you switch back and forth between the different rules is very informative.

You will find that the Hebb rule differs from the others in not producing inhibition. As a consequence it does not select between alternative interpretations of a test pattern, but simply produces a response that is the sum of the two. By contrast the other rules produce a net that chooses the best single interpretation. To see this use a test pattern that is most of one of the two learned characters plus just one feature of the other, and compare the outcomes produced by using each rule.

Characters sharing features.

Click *Options*, then *Clear Patterns*, then have the net learn two new patterns sharing a feature, e.g. a 4 and a K. Again try various test patterns with each of the rules.

Question: You will find that in this case only one of the rules produces weights that reliably completes partial inputs, removes additional elements, and chooses the learned character that shares most features with the input. Which is it? Why do the others fail?

Program Three: Build your own Hebbian net

This program allows you to choose the size of the net up to a maximum of 25 units, to specify system parameters, to input patterns from a file, or to generate new patterns at random, and to evaluate the net's performance under each of the learning rules. A procedure is added to make it easier to present learned patterns to the net at test time. A specified percentage of the connections can be lesioned, i.e. fixed at zero, to study the fault tolerance of the net. The experienced user will find this the most useful program for investigating auto-association using Hebbian rules.

How to use the program

It is used in much the same way as Program Two but allows you more control.
1. You begin by specifying how many units you want.
2. The values of three weight change parameters can be set: *Wt Inc++*, *Wt Inc--* and *Wt Dec*. To do this click *Options* then the appropriate parameter. *Wt Inc++* specifies the amount of increase that occurs in all rules when both pre-synaptic and post-synaptic units are active. *Wt Inc--* specifies the amount of increase that occurs in the Covariance rule when both units are inactive. *Wt Dec* specifies the amount of decrease that occurs when one unit is active and the other is not, i.e. in the pre-synaptic rule when the pre-synaptic unit is active but not the post-synaptic unit; in the post-synaptic rule. when the post-synaptic unit is active but not the pre-synaptic unit; and in the Covariance rule when either is active when the other is not.
3. The Hebb rule is not made directly available, but can be implemented by setting both *Wt Inc--* and *Wt Dec* to zero. The value specified for *Wt Inc++* then becomes the learning rate using any of the three rules.
4. A pattern set to be learned can be input directly using the mouse as in Program Two, can be generated at random, or can be input from file. For direct input click *Learn* and then specify the input. To generate new patterns at random click *Random*, and specify the proportion of units to be active before clicking *Learn*. Each click on *Learn* will then bring in a new random pattern. To bring in a file of patterns to be learned click *Filer In* and then type the file name on the keyboard, in CAPITALS, ending with a carriage return. Each click on *Learn* will then bring in the next pattern from the file.

Random takes precedence over the *Filer* so some patterns can be input from file, and then random patterns can be input by setting the random parameter to the required value. Having done this it is not then possible to switch back to input from the file.

When the end of an input file is reached you can then continue to input directly using the mouse.

5. To save the current learned pattern set for later use click *Filer Out*, specify the file name on the keyboard in CAPITALS, and end with a carriage return.
6. To present patterns for test click *Test*. You will then be asked whether you wish to *Verify*? If you wish to specify test inputs as in Program One using the mouse click *No*. If you wish to present just the learned patterns for test click *Yes* then specify the strength of these test input patterns. The net will then be presented with whichever learned input the pointer is aimed at. To exit this test procedure click the centre button as usual.
7. To set a proportion of the learned weights to zero click *Options* then *Lesion* and specify the proportion of weights to be zeroed.
8. To pass the activations generated by processing one test input over into the next test input click *Options* then *Retain Act* at the end of the first test input and before specifying the next test input.
9.) The matrix of weights produced by each learning rule can be displayed by clicking the required rule. Learning does not have to be repeated separately for each rule.

Exercises 1: The basic properties of auto-associative memories

These exercises are designed to illustrate the basic properties and limitations of auto-associative nets. They will also be useful for studying some of the later programs. You should also invent tests of your own to explore the properties of these nets for yourself.
Note: Throughout the following exercises use the pre-synaptic learning rule and the default parameter settings unless told otherwise.

Familiarity and amplification: Learned patterns will be amplified

First select an 11-unit net. Then teach it two patterns e.g. 1 2 3 4 and 4 5 6 7. Test by presenting one of the two learned patterns with each input value set to 0.1. It is best in this case to specify the test patterns yourself using the mouse, so say *No* to *Verify*? Watch the output activations carefully as the internal interactions are cycled on test. As the units that are active in each pattern support each other their activations will go on increasing until they reach a maximum. This happens within about four or five test cycles. Testing in the same way with unlearned patterns, e.g. 8 9 10 11 in this case, will show that they are not amplified. Familiarity thus determines how rapidly the output of the net grows, so amplification could be used as a signal that the input pattern is familiar.

Amplification may also be useful for figure-ground separation. Test with units 4 to 11 all set to 0.1 to see this. Amplification will cause the outputs for the familiar pattern to rise, and in this example the background activity will be suppressed.

Question: When testing with a weak input of one of the two learned patterns, one of the elements is amplified more rapidly than the others; which is it and why?

Short-term memory: Learned patterns will be maintained

If the net is presented with one of the learned patterns then it will continue to output that pattern after the input is removed. The connections within the net will maintain unit activity. To see this use a net that has learned some patterns, e.g. the two patterns of the preceding exercise, then present a test input of one of the learned patterns at a strength of 0.1 using direct mouse input (i.e. not by verifying). Present just a single test cycle and exit the test procedure. Click *Options* then *Retain Act*. This removes the current external test input but retains all the internal activations. Click *Continue*, then *Test*, then *No*. Now present a test input with no active units. This will show that the internal activation of the net alone continues to amplify and then maintain the previously presented pattern. It is worth repeating this exercise using an initial test input of units 4 to 11 all set to 0.1.

Note that *Retain Act* automatically switches to Off after each time it is used.

Long-term memory implemented as weight changes in a distributed memory therefore has as a natural consequence a mechanism for the short-term maintenance of familiar patterns. Indeed, the mechanism is so good that unless there is some way of turning it off the net will simply continue producing the same familiar pattern of activity until new inputs make it change.

Content-addressable memory: A novel pattern of activity will tend to evolve into the familiar pattern to which it is most similar

This is one of the most important properties of auto-associative memories. It is the one that enables them to act as content addressable memories. The net can reconstruct the whole of a memory from parts of it. This reconstruction can occur very rapidly because it does not involve any serial searching through the set of all learned patterns.

One of the simplest examples of this property is a net with two quite distinct learned states. For example, use an 8-unit net and teach it the patterns 1 2 3 4 and 5 6 7 8. When you test the net with various inputs you will see that nearly all will develop into one of the two learned patterns or the other, i.e., start states are attracted to these two end states. These are therefore called the attractor states of the net (see Tank and Hopfield (1987) for a simple but authoritative introduction). As the net in this example has only two learned patterns it tends to function as a flip-flop. The net can of course have more than two attractor states depending on how it has been trained.

Only one or two test cycles, or relaxation cycles, are needed to reach one of the two end states for many of the possible test inputs. For some it can be longer, however. To see this try test inputs where both patterns get a total input activity of 1.0, but distributed across the units of the two patterns in different ways, e.g. 0.1, 0.2, 0.3, 0.4, 0.2, 0.2, 0.2, 0.4.

Question: How many relaxation cycles are required for the net to reach a stable state in this last example? Which familiar pattern wins, and why?

This exercise illustrates both pattern completion and error correction. Pattern completion occurs where the test pattern is a familiar pattern with parts missing. Error correction occurs when the test pattern has extra parts. These nets can handle both cases, and therefore they provide fast error-correcting content addressable memory. This is a capability that conventional computing cannot efficiently provide.

Many variations on this exercise are possible, with more learned patterns, and with patterns that share features. You should invent some for yourself using larger nets and more patterns. You will find that these nets can develop rich and complex patterns of attractor states, that the attractors depend upon the training input, and that this relation is not simply a matter of always making each input pattern into an attractor state. Consideration of the potential computational value of these properties raises a variety of issues, the most important of which are studied in the following exercises.

Abstraction: Regularities in the associations between inputs are automatically learned

Input patterns that have active units in common will affect common synapses. Synaptic connection strengths will therefore learn some of the regularities that apply across different input patterns. Units that are usually on together will excite each other, ones that are rarely on together will inhibit each other.

One example of this is prototype extraction. To see this in a simple form use a 10-unit net. Assume two underlying prototypes: 1 2 3 4 and 7 8 9 10. Assume also that units 5 and 6 are just noisy units that are sometimes on and sometimes off, and that the net never sees the whole of each prototype. This produces the following training set:

Pattern 1:	1 2 3 5
2:	1 2 4 6
3:	1 3 4
4:	2 3 4
5:	5 7 8 9
6:	6 7 8 10
7:	7 9 10
8:	8 9 10

This pattern set is in data file PROT10H (short for prototypes in a 10-unit Hebbian net). To prepare this set for learning click *Filer In*, and specify this file. Clicking *Learn* will then present patterns from this set in turn. When all 8 patterns have been learned test using *Verify* with a strength of 0.1. You will see that when tested with each of the originally presented patterns the net reconstructs and amplifies the prototype from which that pattern was generated rather than just the original pattern itself. Furthermore, it does this even though it has never seen the prototype during training. Thus the net generates just two attractors, not eight. Many variations on this exercise are possible. For experiments showing similar phenomena in human prototype learning see Posner and Keele (1970) and Knapp and Anderson (1984).

An important consequence of abstraction is feature discovery. To see this in a simple form, select an 8 unit net and have it learn the following four patterns: 1 2 5 6; 1 2 7 8; 3 4 5 6; 3 4 7 8. You will see that the net learns which units are always on together, i.e. the excitatory connections, and which units are never on together, i.e. the inhibitory connections. Connections between the different feature values are neutral because all possible combinations across features occur with equal frequency. Testing will show that for nearly all test patterns the net's output is in keeping with these abstractions.

This exercise can be seen as an example of how a net can build macro-features from micro-features. Units 1 2 3 4 specify one value of a feature having just two possible values, and units 5 6 7 8 do likewise, i.e. (1+2 or 3+4) and (5+6 or 7+8). With just two binary valued features there are only four possible patterns, and the net sees each of them. Real patterns will have many more macro-features than this, and each feature will often have more than just two possible values. If the macro-features are reliably composed from the micro-features then that structure will be discovered by the net.

Biological neural systems will usually be presented with just a tiny sub-set of all the possible patterns that could be formed from the feature domain. The following exercise therefore studies the ability of auto-associative nets to learn which particular patterns it has seen from the set of all those that are possible.

Capacity and the interaction between patterns: Many specific patterns can be learned but capacity is limited by the interaction between different patterns

Assessment of the capacity of neural nets to learn various sets of patterns raises unresolved and complex issues. One approach is to see how many patterns the net can store reliably before interference between different patterns occurs. This is not as straightforward as it sounds, because reliable storage can be defined in various ways, and because the answer depends in complex ways upon the learning rule and the relations between the patterns learned. We make no attempt to resolve these issues here. Our goal is simply to alert the reader to some of them, and to show some ways in which they can be studied.

An important issue that has concerned psychologists is whether these nets can remember specific things as well as generalisations. For example, we learn many specific spoken words as well as learning the very much smaller set of elementary speech sounds from which all the words are built.

The following exercise illustrates this issue. It assumes that the individual units of the net specify micro-features that only occur in well-specified combinations, and that thus specify the macro-features from which specific items are built.

Use a 24 unit net, the Pre-synaptic Rule, and set *Wt Inc++* to 0.9 and *Wt Dec* to 0.6. (*Wt Inc--* is irrelevant to this rule but should be set to about 0.3 if comparison with the Covariance Rule is intended). Assume six macro-features as follows: (1+2 or 3+4); (5+6 or 7+8); (9+10 or 11+12); (13+14 or 15+16); (17+18 or 19+20); (21+22 or 23+24). Assume also that input patterns can leave some macro-features blank. That is one value or the other or neither value may be activated, e.g. (1+2 or 3+4 or neither). With this feature structure $3^5 - 1$, i.e. 242 specific patterns are possible, excluding the case where all feature values are left blank.

We can now study the ability of the net to learn both the macro-feature structure and a very specific sub-set of the possible patterns. This set is stored in the file STR24H (short for structured patterns in a 24-unit Hebbian net), and contains the following patterns:

Pattern 1:	3 4 7 8 9 10 17 18 23 24
2:	3 4 5 6 9 10 15 16 21 22
3:	7 8 11 12 13 14 19 20
4:	1 2 15 16 19 20
5:	5 6 13 14 21 22
6:	1 2 11 12 17 18 23 24
7:	7 8 13 14 17 18 23 24
8:	3 4 5 6 21 22
9:	9 10 11 12 15 16 19 20

Load this set by clicking *Filer in*, then typing STR24H followed by the return key. Then click *Learn* six times to learn the first six patterns from this set.

Memory for these patterns can now be tested. One way to do this is to use *Verify* with a strength between 0.1 and 0.5. This is an especially informative test because each part of the pattern that is amplified by the net on this test would be reconstructed by the net if that was the only part missing on a completion test. We therefore recommend this as a standard way of testing auto-associative memories.

When just the first six of the above patterns have been presented once each for learning all six are stored reliably in the sense that each is a stable state of the network. This is shown by the fact that the net amplifies these patterns, and does not change any of them into some other pattern when test cycles are iterated.

When learning is extended to include Pattern 7 interference occurs in that Pattern 6 is then no longer a stable state of the network but is changed into Pattern 7. When Patterns 8 and 9 are learned only five are stable states.

Therefore in this case only up to about six specific patterns can be learned as stable states before interference occurs. The abilities and limitations of all three learning rules in this particular case will be found to be very similar. The limitation to six different patterns is severe, but fortunately does not apply to auto-associative memories in general.

It is important to see that the learned patterns are not just stable states, they are also attractor states. They are reconstructed from input states, or retrieval cues, that are to some extent similar to the required final state. The set of initial states from which any particular learned state can be reconstructed is called its attractor basin or catchment area. Testing after just the first seven patterns are learned will show that the size of their attractor basins varies; in this case a weak input of Pattern 3 is transformed into Pattern 7 which has a wider attractor basin. Learned states therefore vary in the variety of cues from which they can be retrieved, as do our own memories.

Even with the system as it is particular patterns can be learned if necessary by presenting them for further learning trials. In our example Pattern 6 is not a stable state of the net after just one presentation of all nine patterns. If Pattern 6 is then presented for just one more learning trial it becomes a stable state, but it does so at the expense of other memories.

The regular feature structure obeyed by all nine patterns can be seen in the pattern of excitatory and inhibitory connections along the main diagonal of the weight matrix. That is, units 1 and 2 excite each other, as do units 3 and 4, but each pair inhibits the other. As a consequence the net will be able to learn new patterns that use this feature structure more easily than it can learn new ones that do not; just as we can learn new words in our own language more easily than we can learn new words in a language that is foreign to us.

We have not yet given any general principles for determining how many patterns nets of this sort can learn. This has often been found to increase regularly with the total number of units in the net (N). Therefore it is often expressed as a proportion of N. The auto-associative nets used by Hopfield (1982) had a capacity of approximately 0.15N. (It is actually the number of connections that ultimately matters (Amit, 1989) but in fully connected nets this will covary with the number of units.)

Capacity is important because higher organisms need to learn many different items. This will not be a problem if capacity increases with N, because any subsystem of the mammalian cortex that functions as an auto-associative memory will have many thousands of neurons. The next example therefore illustrates the relation between net size and memory capacity.

We will compare the number of random patterns that can be learned in 12-unit and 24-unit nets. Use the Covariance rule, with *Wt Inc++*, *Wt Inc--*, and *Wt Dec* all set to 1, their default values. The maximum number of units that can be used in these simulations, 25, is far too small to allow adequate study of the capacity for learning patterns with regular internal structure such as in the preceding exercise. We therefore use random patterns. Even then the size of the nets is still too small to allow the statistical effects that apply to much larger nets to apply reliably. Nevertheless, this exercise provides some evidence that capacity increases with the number of units.

First, use a 24 unit net and click *Filer In* to select the set of five random patterns in the file RAN24H for learning. Click *Learn* until the first four patterns are learned. A verification test at a strength of 0.5 will then show that all four patterns are learned as attractor states of the net. When the next pattern is learned, however, testing will show that one of the five patterns has been disrupted. In this case, therefore, up to four patterns can be learned. As this is a 24 unit net, N = 4/24 = 0.1666N, greater than Hopfield's 0.15N.

The following experiment looks at the reliability of this result across a larger set of random patterns and net sizes. Restart the program. Select a 24 unit net and the Covariance rule. Click *Random* and specify 0.5 as the probability that a unit will be active. Click *Learn* four times to learn four random patterns. Do a verification test at 0.5 and note the number of bit errors in the output of the net after at least 10 relaxation cycles for each of the four patterns. Click *Options* then *Clear Patterns* and repeat the above five or ten times. From the results calculate the average number of patterns out of four stored without error, and the average number of bits stored out of the maximum of 96 (4 x 24). Repeat with a 12 unit net.

Results that we obtained from such an experiment showed that on average a 24 unit net stored 3 out of 4 patterns completely correctly, and stored 85.8 out of 96 bits (4 x 24). A 12 unit net stored 1.6 out of 4 patterns, and 41.1 bits out of 48 bits(4 x 12). Thus doubling the number of units approximately doubled capacity.

These demonstrations show that even these simple nets can learn specific items together with generalisations. They also show that interference between memories can be a major cause of forgetting. Human memory also has these properties. This similarity does not imply that human memory is a simple homogeneous neural net of the sort studied here. There are plenty of very good reasons for supposing that it is far more complex, with internal functional specialisations that are not reflected in the simple structures used here. Nevertheless, these similarities, and others, justify the working assumption that human cognition may be built somehow from structures of this sort.

Fault tolerance: Auto-associative memories are robust

Another similarity of great theoretical and practical importance between these nets and biological memories is their fault tolerance. To enable you to study this we have provided for a specified proportion of the connections to be "lesioned", i.e. set to zero. Click *Options* then *Lesion* and specify the proportion to be affected. Then continue to test. In one study of this property we taught the net the first four patterns of the set RAN24H then successively lesioned 10% of the connections. The first 10% had little effect on performance. Performance degraded gradually with damage rather than precipitously, and even when 40%

of connections were lost the four patterns were still quite well remembered. Connections can be lesioned successively, but note that the random sampling is from all connections, not just previously unlesioned ones.

Exercises 2: Further study of auto-associative nets and Hebbian learning

Associative networks with feedback connections such as those studied here can have very rich patterns of dynamic behaviour, and the analysis of this behaviour goes far beyond what is possible here. This analysis is sufficiently rewarding and difficult to attract the sustained attention of statistical physicists (e.g. Amit, 1989). The nets simulated here are too small for all of these statistical cooperative effects to be demonstrated, but many aspects can be studied, as illustrated by the following two exercises.

The effects of activation density

In our previous examples patterns have had roughly half of their units active. However, much less than half of the cells in associative cortex are active at any one time. Furthermore, Willshaw and Dayan (1990), Nadal and Toulouse (1990), and many others have shown that the storage efficiency of neural nets usually increases as the density of unit activation decreases, i.e. performance is better if activation is sparse.

You should try to work out for yourself ways of testing the effects of activation density on the performance of nets using the Hebb and Pre-synaptic rules.

In contrast to the other rules the Hopfield version of the Covariance rule does not perform well when activation is sparse. For a simple demonstration of the advantage of the Pre-synaptic rule over the Hopfield rule when activation is sparse use a 12-unit net and the default values for the weight change parameters (all equal to 1). Input the five patterns 1 2, 3 4, 5 6, 7 8, 9 10, then test. The Pre-synaptic rule produces five attractor states whereas the Hopfield rule turns the net into a single large attractor. Learning rules that are symmetrical across the "on" and "off" state of the units (such as the Hopfield rule) are thus not suited to patterns with sparse activation. This is because when activation is sparse most units will be "off" most of the time. Therefore they will all tend to become associated with each other.

Optimal settings of the weight change parameters

Willshaw and Dayan (1990) have studied the three rules used here by formal mathematical analysis and by computer simulation. They conclude that these rules are optimal when the weight changes are set to appropriate values that depend upon activation density, p (the probability that units are active). They studied pattern matching nets but generalising their results to auto-associative nets suggests that the Covariance rule is optimal when *Wt Inc++* = $(1\text{-p})^2$, *Wt Inc--* = p^2, and *Wt Dec* = p(1-p); and that the Pre-synaptic and Post-synaptic rules are optimal when *Wt Inc++* = 1-p, and *Wt Dec* = p. They also show that the Covariance rule is the most optimal of the three, but that this advantage is small when activation density, p, is small.

In one study of these relations in our nets we used the Covariance rule in a 25 unit net with random patterns having an activation density of 0.2. Willshaw and Dayan's analysis thus predicts that the optimum values will be *Wt Inc++* = 0.64, *Wt Inc--* = 0.04, and *Wt Dec* = 0.16. In fact, in a purely empirical study, we found that these settings produce a net that is too excitatory, learning only 1.7 out of 8 patterns on average. Using these values except with *Wt Inc++* = 0.36 produced a net that learned 5.5 out of 8 on average. This may be due to the small size of our nets, to the auto-associative architecture, or to the units all having output functions with thresholds that are fixed at zero.

Program Four: Introduction to the Delta rule

This simulation and the one following are modelled on the single-layer auto-associative net described by McClelland and Rumelhart (1985). The program is best used in conjunction with reading that paper (see Appendix Two for a formal specification of the model). The thrust of the paper centres on the fact that people who are shown examples of a particular category can respond faster and more accurately to the prototype of that category (which they may not have seen) than to any examples of the category, but can also learn specific examples. McClelland and Rumelhart suggest that memory must be organised in such a way that it automatically extracts the prototype from the separate examples. They propose that abstraction and the preservation of information about specific stimuli are simply reflections of the same basic learning mechanism.

The basic learning mechanism that they propose is the Delta rule. We have already seen that some Hebbian rules can learn both abstractions and specific stimuli, but that capacity is limited. The Delta rule has a much higher capacity. It is based upon the idea that if the required output for any input is specified then the net can learn by gradually changing the connection strengths so as to reduce the "error", i.e. the difference between what the net is currently producing and what it should be producing. If what it is producing is less than required then connections from active input lines are increased, and if it is more than required then they are decreased. If it is producing exactly the right output then no change is made. It has often been shown by formal mathematical analysis that if a set of connection strengths exists that solves the problem then this procedure will find them, providing that the size of the changes is not too large and that learning goes on for long enough.

The Delta rule is a generalisation of the Perceptron Convergence procedure invented by Frank Rosenblatt, one of the first workers on neural nets in the 1950s. It has been extensively explored because it works well, but it has not so far been based upon any physiological evidence. There is psychological evidence for such a rule, however. It is mathematically very similar to the learning rule that was inferred from a great deal of evidence on associative learning by Rescorla and Wagner (see Sutton and Barto, 1981).

There are two fundamental differences between the Delta rule and Hebbian rules. First, as described at the beginning of this chapter, Hebbian rules use only two terms to determine the change in weights; whereas the Delta rule uses three terms. Second, with Hebbian rules all the weight changes can be made using just one presentation of each stimulus. With the Delta rule the learning procedure must cycle through the whole set of input patterns many times, making small changes to the weights for every pattern in the set. One cycle through the whole set is called an epoch. The amount of the weight change at connections is a small proportion of the difference between the actual and desired post-synaptic activity. This difference, or error, is given the Greek symbol delta, hence the "Delta rule".

There are two other important differences between the Delta net used here and the Hebbian nets. Neither are critical to the operation of the Delta rule, but are included for comparability with the net of McClelland and Rumelhart (1985). First, unit outputs range between -1 and +1, in contrast to the Hebbian rules which use outputs ranging between 0 and 1. The latter is more biologically plausible as there is no evidence that axonal signals can take negative values.

One consequence of using positive and negative outputs is that it affects orthogonality. The general definition of orthogonality is that two patterns are orthogonal if the sum of the products of corresponding units equals zero. A pattern set is then orthogonal if all possible pattern pairings are orthogonal. A simple way to understand orthogonality in the current context is that when the input values range between 0 and 1 orthogonal patterns cannot share active units; when values are either -1 or +1 they must share active units, but corresponding units must be of the same sign as often as they are of opposite sign. Thus, changing they way in which a pair of patterns is coded can change whether they are orthogonal or not, e.g.

	Hebbian Pattern A	Hebbian Pattern B	Delta Pattern A	Delta Pattern B
Unit 1	1	1	+1	+1
Unit 2	0	1	-1	+1
Unit 3	1	0	+1	-1
Unit 4	0	0	-1	-1
Unit 5	1	0	+1	-1
Unit 6	1	1	+1	+1
Unit 7	0	0	-1	-1
Unit 8	0	1	-1	+1
	Non-orthogonal		Orthogonal	

The second difference is that the dynamic change of the net's activation and output in response to input is more complex. On each processing cycle and for each unit the net input is calculated, then the activation is updated. If the net input is positive then activation is incremented by an amount that is proportional to the distance left to the ceiling activation level of +1.0. If net input is negative then activation is decreased by an amount that is proportional to the distance left to the floor activation level of -1.0. These dynamics are controlled by the settings of the *Excite* and *Decay* parameters in a way that will be illustrated in the exercises for Program 5. The *Excite* parameter affects the strength of the net input, and should always be much less than 1. *Decay* determines how close to +1.0 and -1.0 output can go; the smaller its value the closer that output can reach these asymptotic values.

How to use the program

The program is used in much the same way as the introductory program on Hebbian nets. It has two sections. Section One learns a pair of patterns that do not share active units, and which in this case are therefore not orthogonal. Section Two learns a pair of patterns that share half of their active units, and that in this case are orthogonal.

To learn Pattern A click *Learn*. Watch the activations carefully. Then to learn Pattern B click *Continue*. To test click *Test* and specify input as in the Hebbian nets.

To proceed from Section One to Section Two click *Options*, *Quit*, and *Continue to next program.*

Cautionary note: The demonstration may give a false impression of how the Delta rule works on first viewing. In this demonstration pattern A is learned, then pattern B is learned, which allows the user two opportunities to see how the weights are assigned. Pattern A is thus learned on top of the weights for pattern B, resulting in a weights matrix for the two patterns (see also

McClelland and Rumelhart, page 167 for the same pattern set). However it should be clearly understood that the Delta rule usually operates by cycling many times through all the patterns in the pattern set.

Graphical representation of the net

The rationale for changing the weights is to produce a situation where the internal input to each unit has the same effect on that unit as the external input to the unit. The distinction between external and internal is made graphically by providing two lines to each unit, the upper line representing external input and the lower representing internal input. The unit activation level is similarly divided; the upper semicircle represents activation provided by external input, the lower semicircle shows internal input. Learning is the process of making the internal activation the same as the external activation.

Input, output, and unit activation are shown in black for negative values and white (grey) for positive values.

Exercises

Testing will show that the Delta rule does a good job of learning both orthogonal and non-orthogonal pairs of patterns.

The parameters *Excitation*, *Decay* and *Learning* rate can be modified by the user. It is advisable to use the default parameters for the first simulation, then to modify each parameter in turn noting the effect of changes in net performance in terms of number of learning cycles, pattern completion and error correcting capacity. More specific exercises studying these parameters will be given for the following program where a greater variety of net sizes and pattern sets can be used.

Program Five:
Build your own Delta net

The program allows users to set up their own nets and explore the Delta rule in more detail. The program is suitable for more advanced users and is useful for investigation in the same way as Program Three for the Hebbian rules.

How to use the program

This program is used in much the same way as Program Three.
1. You begin by specifying how many units you want.
2. The values of three parameters can be set: *Learning* affects the size of the weight change made during learning. It should usually be small, i.e. less than 0.1. Net input is multiplied by *Excite* to determine the final activation value, which should always be between -1 and +1. *Decay* determines what proportion of the activation from the previous processing cycle is carried over into the current cycle. If *Decay* is 0 then all of it is carried over.
3. A pattern set to be learned can be input directly using the mouse, can be generated at random, or can be input from file, as in Program Three. To generate new patterns at random click *Continue*, then *Random*, and specify the proportion of units to be active, before clicking *Continue* and *Input*. Each click on *Input* will then bring in a new random pattern. To bring in a file of patterns to be learned click *Filer In* and then type the file name on the keyboard, in CAPITALS, ending with a return. Each click on *Input* will then bring in the next pattern from the file.
4. To learn the set of patterns that you have input click *Learn*. This will then run 30 learning epochs. Each further click will then initiate a further 30 epochs. Learning can be stopped by clicking the mouse button. Once a set of patterns has been input, clicking *Options* then *Clear Weights* allows you to change the parameter settings, and then to learn that pattern set again.
Patterns learned are shown in grey and white, but as they are coded using +1 and -1 by the net they are shown as black and white (grey) within the net.
5. To save the current learned pattern set for later use click *Filer Out*, specify the file name on the keyboard in CAPITALS, and end with a carriage return.
6. To present patterns for test click *Test*. You will then be asked whether you wish to *Verify*? If you wish to specify test inputs using the mouse click *No*. If you wish to present just the learned patterns for test click *Yes* then specify the strength of these test input patterns. The net will then be presented with whichever input the mouse pointer is aimed at.
7. To specify an output threshold click *Options*, then *Threshold*. Only activations beyond the specified level will then be output. Then select +- if you want both positive and negative outputs, and + if you want only positive outputs.

Exercises

The following exercises should be run using the default parameter values at least initially. If the inputs to the units becomes too large the net can enter an uncontrolled oscillatory state. Therefore weights should not be allowed to become too big.

Processing dynamics

The way in which activation changes as the net processes an input is more complex than in those used for the Hebbian rules. This greater complexity is not essential to the operation of the Delta rule, but is included for comparability with the net of McClelland and Rumelhart (1985). This exercise is designed to help you get some understanding of these dynamics and the net parameters that control them.

Use a net in which the weights are still all set to zero so that the total input to each unit is determined only by the external input. To do this select a small net, e.g. 4 units. Input a blank pattern but do not learn it; this is simply to provide access to the test routine while the weights are still zero. Now you can see how activation and output evolve, using direct mouse input, together with various values for the *Excite* and *Decay* parameters.

First set *Decay*=0. You will then see that output rises to 1.0 for any input greater than 0, but at a rate determined by IE, (i.e. *Input* X *Excite*). When *Input*=0.1 and *Excite*=0.1 it takes about 250 cycles before output is near to 1.0. When *Input*= 1.0 and *Excite*=0.2 it takes only about 20 cycles.

Next set *Decay* = 0.1, which is the value that we suggest for the following exercises. You will then see that output now rises to a value of less than 1. This value is in fact equal to IE divided by IE+*Decay*. So for positive inputs of 1.0, as in our learned patterns, values for *Excite* of 0.05, 0.1, 0.2 will give outputs of 0.333, 0.5, and 0.667 respectively. You will also see that the output gets close to these values within 30 cycles. During learning therefore many relaxation cycles are run for each pattern in each epoch before the weights are changed. In order to learn a set of just five patterns thousands of cycles may be necessary. This contrasts greatly with the Hebbian nets where only 5 cycles are required.

Basic properties of auto-associative memories

All of the properties demonstrated in the first set of exercises for Program 3 remain true for nets trained with the Delta rule. Most of the exercises suggested there can be repeated here, e.g. amplification, the 8-unit flip-flop, prototype abstraction, and feature discovery.

Data files PROT10D, STR24D, and RAN24D are provided for these exercises. They are equivalent to those provided for the Hebbian nets except that they are coded using +1 and -1 rather than using +1 and 0.

You will find that the detailed behaviour is not always as in the Hebbian nets. One of the reasons for this is that units that are "off" send a negative signal to other units, not no signal as in the Hebbian nets. For every pattern presented the net learns not one but two patterns, the pattern specified by the "on" units, and the pattern specified by the "off" units.

Capacity

Hebbian rules are guaranteed to learn pattern sets that are orthogonal, i.e., that do not share active units. They can learn some pattern sets that are not orthogonal but they are not guaranteed to do so, and have limited capacity. Nets trained with the Delta rule have a much higher capacity. They are guaranteed to learn sets of patterns that are not orthogonal provided that they are linearly independent. That is, provided that the value required for each unit to complete each pattern can be calculated from just the sum of the activities of the other units multiplied by the weight on their connection to the unit. That calculation, after all, is just the one that the units perform.

To see the higher capacity of the Delta rule first learn the set RAN24D. This is the same pattern set as RAN24H, except coded as "-1"s and "+1"s instead of as "0"s and "1"s. You will see that the Delta rule can learn all five patterns, whereas the Hebbian rules learned only the first four. You can then explore the capacity of the Delta rule in 12 an 24 unit nets using the option for generating new random pattern sets, and compare that with the results obtained with Hebbian nets.

Activation density

Activation density does not have the same effects in this net as in the Hebbian nets. As "off" elements send negative signals to other units they are in a sense on. Exploring these effects will show that such a design is not only biologically implausible but introduces counter-intuitive behaviour of doubtful value.

As an example, try the test used in Exercise 2 of Program 3, in which a 12-unit net is trained with the five patterns 1 2, 3 4, 5 6, 7 8, 9 10.

Output threshold

The effects of having negative outputs can to some extent be investigated using the *Threshold* option. Selecting + rather than +/- will limit the outputs at test to positive values only.

McClelland and Rumelhart exercises

There are a number of interesting examples in McClelland and Rumelhart (1985), particularly those showing prototype extraction. These examples can be tried in our net, but remember that they usually set *Excite*=0.15, *Decay*=0.15. and *Learning*=0.85/(N-1), where N=number of units in net, whereas with our net we find more reliable performance with smaller values, e.g. *Learning* = 0.01 for a 24 unit net.

Suggestions for further reading

Hinton and Anderson (1981) first introduced associative nets to a wide psychological audience, and still provides a good starting point, particularly the introductory chapter by Hinton and Anderson. It has recently been reissued in a revised version. The PDP Volumes of Rumelhart and McClelland (1986) are also considered to be classic introductions. Part I of Volume 1, and Chapter 17 of Volume 2 are particularly relevant to this chapter. Kohonen (1987) provides a useful survey of associative memories for the mathematically sophisticated.

6

Pattern Association

Auto-associative nets are designed to store and retrieve individual patterns. Pattern associators are designed to associate output patterns with input patterns. Training consists of presenting pairs of patterns, rather than just single patterns. Testing consists of presenting an input pattern and examining the output pattern produced.

The performance of pattern associators can be seen as a simple analogy to stimulus-response learning in animals, where the input of one pattern (the stimulus) produces the output of another pattern (the response).
The architecture of a basic pattern associator consists of a set of input units and a set of output units. All output units are connected to all input units with weights at connections, as in Figure 6.1.

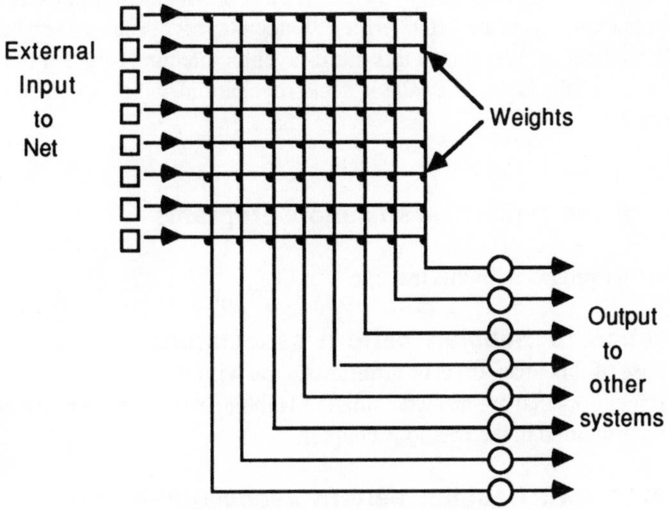

Figure 6.1. A single-layer pattern associator

Representation and learning are the same as in the auto-associators. Inputs and outputs are patterns of activation across a population of units. Two-term (Hebbian) and three-term (Delta) learning rules can be applied to pattern associators and are available in this module.

The abilities and limitations of pattern associators are thus similar to those of auto-associators. The main difference is that the processing of inputs is very much simpler in pattern associators because they have only feed-forward connections. The rich patterns of dynamic behaviour produced in auto-associative nets by the feed-back connections do not occur. For example, pattern associators do not produce outputs that gradually evolve towards a steady state, or that oscillate. The input can specify the output in one processing cycle, and that is all there is to it. Of course, the way in which information is passed from input to output can be made to build up gradually over time, but that will not change the outcome. Thus, if you have got the basic ideas of the previous chapter then pattern association will be easy to understand.

Nets with the architecture of Figure 6.1 are often called single layer nets. This may sound strange as there are two layers of units. The reason for this terminology is that although there are two layers of units there is only one layer of weights, and this limits what the net can do. The activity required from each output unit must be predictable by just adding together the activities of the input units multiplied by the weights on the connections from them. This means that the input units must be treated as independent sources of information; outputs cannot be calculated on the basis of relations between the input units. The final exercise suggested for Program Four will illustrate this limitation. It can be overcome by inserting one or more layers of units between the input and output units. These extra layers are often termed "hidden layers" because they have no external connections. Weights in this multi-layer architecture can be trained by a generalisation of the Delta rule called "backpropagation" which will be dealt with in Chapter 7.

Outline of the pattern association programs

There are four programs in this module:

Introduction to Hebbian pattern associators

The purpose of this program is to familiarise you with the basic design of pattern associators that are trained using the Hebbian rules. These rules have already been studied in the previous chapter.

Build your own Hebbian pattern associator

Experienced users will find this the best program for studying Hebbian rules in pattern associating nets. The nets can have up to 10 input units and 10 output units, and can be trained with up to 18 input-output pairs.

Introduction to Delta pattern associators

The purpose of this program is to make clear some of the basic capabilities of the Delta rule in a pattern associating architecture. It will show how the net can learn both regularities in the associations between inputs and outputs, and exceptions to those regularities. The regularity used is the "Rule of 7 and 8", which McClelland and Rumelhart (1986) propose as a simple analogy to the regularities determining the formation of the past tense in English.

Build your own Delta pattern associator

Experienced users will find this the best program for studying the Delta rule in pattern associators. The nets can have up to 10 input units and 10 output units, and can be trained with up to 18 input-output pairs.

Program One: Introduction to Hebbian pattern associators

This program operates in a similar way to the introductory auto-associative program, and has only limited flexibility. It provides a serial stepping procedure through each of two sets of patterns to allow users to note how the input and output patterns and the learning rule determine the resulting connectivity matrix. Note however, that a pattern associator is a parallel processing device and the artificial serial procedure is used only for exposition.

The learning rules, and most of the operating procedures, are the same as in Chapter Five, with which we assume the reader to be familiar. The test procedure for pattern associators uses only one pass through the net, unlike the auto-associators which cycle activation around the net.

How to use the program

The operating procedures are similar to those for the introductory program on auto-associators. The main steps are as follows.

1. Select a learning rule.
2. Repeatedly click *Learn* to learn the first pair of patterns. The pathways from pre-synaptic input unit to each post-synaptic output unit will then be highlighted. To make it easier for you to note how the weights are assigned at each connection they are highlighted for each output unit in turn.
3. Again click *Continue* and *Learn* to learn the second pattern pair.
4. Click *Test* and then present input patterns to test the net's response. Select units and specify their strength of activity using the mouse pointer as in the auto-associative programs

Exercises

The Hebb rule

First use the Hebb rule. Note that it simply copies the pattern of active input units into excitatory weights to those output units that are active. Test using weak input patterns and partial input patterns. Also present an input pattern that is all or most of one of the original stimulus patterns plus a small part of one of the others or of one of the two unused input units.

The Stent-Singer rule

Note that like the Hebb rule this rule copies the active input units into excitatory weights to the active output units, but also copies the inactive input units into inhibitory weights to the active output units. As for the Hebb rule test using weak, partial and mixed input patterns. You will find that the main difference from the Hebb rule is that this rule does not give both of the two learned responses to tests that combine parts of the two original stimuli. Instead it gives the response that was paired with the stimulus that is most strongly present in the test input.

The Hopfield rule

In this case all of the weights are changed when each of the two patterns is learned. Test as before using weak, partial, and mixed patterns. You will find that this differs from the Stent-Singer rule mainly in how it treats units that were inactive during training.

Program Two: Build your own Hebbian pattern associator

How to use the program

This program is operated in much the same way as Program 3 of the Auto-associators.

1. You begin by specifying how many units you want in the input and output layers.

2. The values of four weight change parameters can be set: *Wt Inc++*, *Wt Inc--*, *Wt Dec+-*, *and Wt Dec-+*. To do this click *Options* then the appropriate parameter. *Wt Inc++* specifies the amount of increase that occurs in all rules when both pre- and post-synaptic units are active. *Wt Inc--* specifies the amount of increase that occurs in the covariance rule when both units are inactive. *Wt Dec+-* specifies the amount of decrease that occurs when the pre-synaptic unit is active but the post-synaptic is not. *Wt Dec-+* specifies the amount of decrease that occurs when the post-synaptic unit is active but the pre-synaptic unit is not.

3. The Hebb rule is not made directly available, but can be implemented by setting all parameters except *Wt Inc ++* to zero. The value specified for *Wt Inc++* then becomes the learning rate using any of the three rules.
4. A pattern set to be learned can be input directly using the mouse, can be generated at random, or can be input from file. To input directly click *Learn* and then specify the patterns. To generate new patterns at random simply click *Random*, and specify the proportion of units to be active, before clicking *Learn*. Each click on *Learn* will then bring in a new random pattern. To bring in a file of patterns to be learned click *Filer In* and then type the file name on the keyboard, in CAPITALS, ending with a carriage return. Each click on *Learn* will then bring in the next pattern from the file.
5. To save a pattern set for later use click *Filer Out*, and specify the file name on the keyboard, in CAPITALS, ending with a carriage return.
6. To present patterns for test click *Test*. You will then be asked whether you wish to *Verify*? If you wish to specify test inputs as in Program One using the mouse click *No*. If you wish to present just the learned patterns for test click *Yes*, then specify the strength of these test input patterns. The net will then be presented with the input part of the pair at which the mouse is pointing.
7. The weight matrix produced by each learning rule can be displayed just by clicking the required rule. Learning does not have to be repeated separately for each rule.

Exercises

Many exercises are possible. The following suggestions are intended to help you get started. Use the default weight change parameters unless told otherwise.

Basic comparison of the three rules

To see the basic differences between the three rules select a net with 4 input (layer 1) and 4 output (layer 2) units. Train with just one pattern pair: 1,2 to 1,2. Presenting this pair two or three times will make the weights larger and therefore clearer. Compare the weights generated using each rule. You will see that with the Post-synaptic rule only weights *to* active units change; with the Pre-synaptic rule only weights *from* active units change; with the Covariance rule all change. Repeat this with just one of the four weight change parameters in turn set to 0.1, and study the effect on the weight matrix. The effects are quite simple, and you should try to understand them.

Learning to connect many different inputs to the same output

It is often the case that many different stimuli can lead to the same response. For example, very many different integers can lead to the responses "odd"or "even". As a simple example of how these nets deal with such a requirement specify a net with 8 input and 2 output units. Assume that the first output unit stands for "odd" and the second for "even". Train the net with the first six pairings, i.e. 1 to 1; 2 to 2; 3 to 1; 4 to 2; 5 to 1; 6 to 2.

Comparison of the weights produced by each of the three rules should show that the Covariance and Pre-synaptic rules work well, producing weights that excite the right response and inhibit the wrong response. Note, however, that this is not an example of concept abstraction. What has been learned does not generalise to new inputs, e.g. to units 7 and 8 in this case. This limitation is not due to the learning rules, but to the representation of each distinct input by a single input unit, i.e. a "grandmother-cell" representation.

The Post-synaptic rule does not perform well in connecting many inputs to each output, and produces a wholly inhibitory net. This rule forms excitatory connections to a unit only from units that are reliably on when it is. It will thus be useful where we wish to develop few rather than many alternative inputs. A Post-synaptic rule will be used in such a role in Chapter 8 which deals with the establishment of receptive fields by competitive learning.

The preceding case was perhaps over-simplified because integers can be classified in many different ways, and a much larger output net will be required. For a task that is a little less simple try the "odd-even large-small" problem. Use a net with 8 input and 8 output units. Assume that the first two output units have the same meaning as before, that the third output unit stands for "small", i.e. less than or equal to 4, that the fourth stands for "large", i.e. greater than 4, and that the other output units stand for other possible responses. Train with all eight input-output pairs, i.e. 1 to 1,3; 2 to 2,3; 3 to 1,3; and so on. The full training set is data file NUMB8-8 (short for numbers in an 8 into 8 unit net). Testing and examination of the weights will both show that only the Pre-synaptic rule works well. The Covariance rule produces a net that does not work well because it is too excitatory. A way of overcoming this is shown in the following exercise.

Optimal settings of the weight change parameters

As already discussed in Chapter 5, Willshaw and Dayan (1990) have studied this issue. Their analysis was specifically concerned with pattern-associating nets, and shows that the optimal settings depend upon the proportion, p, of units active in the input patterns, and the proportion, r, of units active in the output patterns.

For the Covariance rule (which they also call Rule 1) this dependence is *Wt Inc*++=(1-p)(1-r), *Wt Inc*--=pr, *Wt Dec*+-=(1-p)r, and *Wt Dec*-+= p(1-r).

For the Post-synaptic rule (their Rule 2) *Wt Inc*++=1-p, *Wt Dec*-+=p (the other two parameters are zero).

For the Pre-synaptic rule (their Rule 3) *Wt Inc*++=1-r, *Wt Dec*+-=r (the other two parameters are zero).

This predicts that the Covariance rule will work optimally when *Wt Inc*++=0.65625, *Wt Inc*--=0.03125, *Wt Dec*+-=0.21875, and *Wt Dec*-+=0.09375 in the "odd-even large-small" problem of the previous exercise. If you repeat that exercise using values close to these you will find that the performance of the Covariance rule is considerably improved.

Another way to explore this issue is to use a 10 into 10 net and the facility for generating random patterns. You could use active proportions of .5 and .3, and set the weight change parameters to values appropriate to these proportions and the rule operating, using the formulae given above. With such small nets one appropriate measure is the average number of bit errors per pattern over sets of four pattern pairs at a time. As variance will be high the averaging should be over at least 10 blocks of four pairs each. Use of the verify procedure will speed testing, and for simplicity any amount of activity in an output unit should be counted as "on".

Concept abstraction

In exercise 4 of Chapter 5 we showed how auto-associative nets can abstract the regular prototype underlying a set of varied noisy instances. This task can be repeated here except that the output units will be told how to classify each exemplar. Thus this may be seen as an example of supervised prototype learning, whereas in the auto-associative case it was unsupervised. The two prototypes assumed in that earlier exercise were the units 1 2 3 4 and the units 5 6 7 8 in a 10-unit net. The training set used in that exercise paired with their appropriate output classifications are in the data file PROT10-2 (short for prototypes in a 10 into 2 net).

Use a 10 into 2 net, and use *Filer In* to load PROT10-2. Select the Pre-synaptic rule then click *Learn* eight times to learn the eight pairs in this file. Testing will then show that all exemplars are correctly classified and that this generalises to new exemplars, e.g. inputs with only two of the four prototypical units active. Furthermore, the net responds more strongly to the whole prototype, which it has not seen during training, than to any of the examples that it has seen. One way to see this effect is to test with all input activations equal to 0.1, but a clearer way is to present an input that is the whole prototype of one class plus a seen exemplar of the other.

An important consequence of prototype abstraction is that new learning that contradicts the abstractions is made more difficult, and achieving it involves modifications to the abstractions. To see this you can use the data file CONT10-2 (short for contradictory exemplars in a 10 into 2 net). The first seven input-output pairs in this file are the same as in PROT10-2, but the eighth pairing replaces 7 8 9 to 2, with 7 8 9 to 1. You will find that this last pairing is no longer learned in just one presentation, but requires an extra two presentations using the Pre-synaptic rule (and more using the Covariance rule). The final pairing is given six times in the file CONT10-2 so that you can make these additional presentations.

If you test after each additional presentation of the contradictory example you will find that as soon as it is learned the response that the net gives to the underlying prototype is changed.

This exercise can be repeated using the two other rules. Each rule combines experiences in its own way, and the Pre-synaptic rule may be best suited to this particular task of prototype abstraction.

This exercise may be seen as a simple analogy to the way our concepts are modified by new learning. New experience that contradicts previous abstractions is hard to assimilate. When accommodation to the new experience is achieved that changes the underlying abstractions. For example, if a child learns to call animals that live in the sea "fish", then it will be harder to learn that dolphins are mammals and not fish. When that is learned then it will change the underlying concept of fish.

A pattern set that Hebbian rules cannot learn

All Hebbian rules associate units on the basis of the correlations between their activations, or the conditional probability of activity in one given activity in the other. Many of our exercises using these rules have shown that this can produce useful computational capabilities. As an example of one limit on these capabilities McClelland and Rumelhart (1988), page 85, give a pattern set that cannot be learned by these rules. This pattern is in the data file HARD4-1. To use it first select a net with 4 input and 1 output unit. Then use *Filer In* to load this pattern. This set of four input-output pairings can be presented twice to make the weights easier to see, so click *Learn* 8 times to present the whole file.

Examination of the resulting weights and verification testing will both show that none of the Hebbian learning rules can learn this set. The reason for this is that the correlations between input and output unit activity are inadequate to produce the required responses. McClelland and Rumelhart emphasise this problem because although Hebbian rules cannot solve it the Delta rule can, and in a pattern-associating net without hidden units. The following two programs therefore explore the design and capabilities of Delta pattern associators.

Program Three: Introduction to Delta pattern associators

One of the best known, and most debated, of all connectionist models of cognition is the use of a pattern associator trained by the Delta rule to learn how to form the past tense of verbs in English (Rumelhart and McClelland, 1986). Early in language development children face the task of having to learn how to form the past tense of a large number of verbs. Verbs such as "to be", "to go", "to have", and "to do" occur frequently so it is essential that children learn these early on. The problem is that many of these verbs have past tenses that are irregular, i.e., they do not form the past tense in the same way as "to want" (wanted), "to walk" (walked), "to smile" (smiled), and so on. The great advantage of regular verbs is that learning a small number of rules greatly facilitates the correct assignment of the past tense ending. Children have to learn both the rules and the exceptions without knowing initially which verbs are regular and which are not. The way in which the rules and the exceptions are represented in the brain is not understood, but McClelland and Rumelhart propose a model which learns both rules and exceptions as a distributed representation in the weights matrix of a pattern associator. To illustrate the basic principles of their theory they invented a simple task requiring the learning of both rules and exceptions. The task involves mapping activity in an 8-unit input layer into activity in an 8-unit output layer. One of the rules governing this mapping is that input unit 7 is mapped into output unit 8, and vice versa. All other input units are mapped into the same number output unit. The rule is therefore called the rule of 7 and 8. Not all mappings follow this rule however. One exception is included, in this case it was that the input 147 maps into 147, and not into 148 as specified by the rule. Readers should consult the original articles, and those of their critics, some of which are listed at the end of this chapter.

How to use the program

Program operation is simple, and involves inputing some or all of the pattern pairs in an internal file containing 18 pairs, and then initiating learning.
1. To prepare a set of patterns for learning click *Input* until the number of patterns to be learned has been loaded. To learn that set click *Learn*. Learning will then proceed until error is below 0.02 for each pattern pair, or until 100 epochs have been reached, or until you click to signal exit.
2. A sub-set of the 18 pattern pairs can be loaded by clicking *Input* and learning initiated, then others can be loaded and learning restarted.
3. The learning rate parameter can be specified by clicking *Learning*. The larger this parameter the quicker the learning, but the less reliable.
4. To change the unit transfer function from logistic to linear or back again click

Output Fn. McClelland and Rumelhart's past tense learning model used a logistic rather than a linear output function. Further information on these functions is given in the PDP books (see especially Volume 2, pp 223- 233).
5. Note that each time the weight matrix is cleared before learning is commenced, the weights are not set to zero, but are randomly set to small values with a mean of zero. Different runs of the same exercise will therefore rarely lead to exactly the same results.
6. To test click *Test* and input the test pattern using the mouse as usual, then click *Continue* to continue learning or testing.

Exercises

Just the simplest exercises will be suggested here. Other exercises are best done using the following program, which has greater flexibility.

Learning regularities and exceptions

First load all 18 patterns by clicking *Input* 18 times. Then initiate learning by clicking *Learn.* When the error is below criterion the learning will stop automatically. If you use the default learning rate this should be in less than 100 epochs, but will take longer if the learning rate is set to a smaller value. If learning does not reach criterion by 100 epochs then it will stop automatically. It can then be restarted by clicking *Learn* again, and letting it run until criterion is reached. Testing will then show that the rule has been learned, and generalises to new instances, and that the exception has also been learned.

Examination of the weight matrix will show how this has been achieved. The input that has to be treated exceptionally is 1 4 7, which goes to 1 4 7 rather than to 1 4 8. What has happened is that the weights from input units 1 and 4 to the output unit 7 have been made sufficiently excitatory to overcome the strong direct excitatory connection from input unit 7 to output unit 8 which results from the regularity. The connections from the input units 2, 3, 5, and 6 to output unit 8 have been strengthened to counterbalance the strong excitatory connections from units 1 and 4 to 7 so that the latter is only effective when the complete item 1 4 7 is presented.

If you carefully watch the error score on the exceptional item, which is the second of the 18 pattern pairs, while this learning occurs you will see that it reduces smoothly throughout the whole course of the learning. This does not agree with the course of past tense learning in children because in that case errors on the irregular verbs are initially low, then increase for a time, and then decrease again. To handle this McClelland and Rumelhart presented items for learning in the way illustrated in the following exercise.

Early learning experiences

Restart the program. Click *Input* twice to input two patterns where the first is regular and the second not.These two pattern pairs are:

2 5 8 --> 2 5 7
1 4 7 --> 1 4 7

The 2 5 8 --> 2 5 7 pair is an example of the “rule’” that input patterns ending in 8 are associated with output patterns ending in 7, and vice-versa. The second pair is an exception to this. These two pairs are intended to be analogous to children’s early learning experience where exceptions to the past tense rules are common, and rules have not yet been learned.

Click *Learn*, and learning will then proceed until criterion is reached, which should take only a few epochs. The error scores and testing will now show that both items have been learned.

Now click *Input* another 16 times to bring in the rest of the pattern set, then click *Learn* to restart learning. You will then see that the error on the exceptional item increases markedly, and then decreases gradually, until again the rules and the exception are both learned.

As an analogy to the course of language learning the sudden extension of the data base used in this example is of course far too abrupt. But it does make the point that extensions of the data base can increase errors on previously correct irregular items in such a connectionist system.

Program Four: Build your own Delta pattern associator

As usual, this “Build your own” program is designed for users to experiment with, and to discover for themselves what each type of net is “good” at, and where the inadequacies of the particular neurocomputational system lie. This program allows you to build a net with up to 10 input and 10 output units, receiving a maximum of 18 pattern pairs. The final exercise suggested shows one of the best known limitations of single-layer nets.

How to use the program

The program is used in much the same way as previous programs. However, unit outputs range between 0 and 1 so, in contrast to the Delta auto-association net in Chapter 5, outputs never become negative.

1. Begin by specifying how many units you want in the input and output layers.
2. The value of the learning rate parameter can be set by clicking *Learning*. It

can be changed at any time during program use. To change parameters while the program is cycling through its learning stage exit using the mouse button(s), change parameters, then return to learning by clicking *Learn*. The learning cycle will continue from the interrupt.

3. A pattern set to be learned can be input directly using the mouse, can be generated at random, or can be input from file. To generate new patterns at random click *Continue*, then *Random*, and specify the proportion of units to be active, before clicking *Continue* and *Input*. Each click on *Input* will then bring in a new random pattern. To bring in a file of patterns to be learned click *Filer In* and then type the file name on the keyboard, in CAPITALS, ending with a return. Each click on *Input* will then bring in the next pattern from the file.

4. To learn the set of patterns that you have input click *Learn*. This will then run learning epochs until successful, or until 100 epochs have been reached. It will continue beyond 100 epochs if *Learn* is again clicked. Learning can be stopped at any time by clicking the mouse button (s).

5. To save a pattern set for later use click *Filer Out*, and specify the file name on the keyboard, in CAPITALS, ending with a carriage return.

6. To present patterns for test click *Test*. You will then be asked whether you wish to *Verify*? If you wish to specify test inputs using the mouse click *No*. If you wish to present just the learned patterns for test click *Yes* then specify the strength of these test input patterns. The net will then be presented with whichever learned input the mouse pointer is aimed at. To exit click the mouse button(s) as usual.

7. To change the unit output function from logistic to linear or back again click *Output Fn*.

8. During learning the error for any specific pair can be seen by moving the pointer controlled by the mouse to the desired pair. Remember the error is the difference between the output produced by the net and the output specified by the training signal.

Exercises

All the exercises suggested for the Hebbian pattern associators can be run using the Delta rule. You will find that the Delta rule can solve all of the problems that the Hebbian rules can, but sometimes requires more learning trials.

Learning time with the Delta rule is very sensitive to the learning rate parameter. Learning is often faster the larger this parameter. In many of the following exercises it can be set to 1.0, but in some others this is too large, and results in the system getting stuck so that it never learns to solve the problem. Using a linear output function for the units rather than a logistic function can also sometimes speed learning, but more often it results in the system not being able to solve the problem at all. You are therefore advised to use the logistic function in the following exercises, unless told otherwise.

An analogy to Kamin Blocking

Kamin is an experimental psychologist who discovered an important phenomenon in associative learning that is seen in a very wide range of species. This phenomenon involves learning trials that pair a compound stimulus, S1+S2, with a response, and then testing to see whether each stimulus alone produces the response. If neither stimulus has previously been been paired with the response then the compound learning trials establish an association between each stimulus separately and the response. However, if an association between one of the two stimuli and the response has already been learned then they will not. That is, the prior learning associating S1 to the response blocks the S2 response association that would otherwise be formed by the compound learning trials.

To see an analogous effect in these nets you can use a net with 8 input and 8 output units. Assume that S1 is activity in input units 1 2 3 4, that S2 is activity in input units 5 6 7 8, and that the response is activity in output units 1 2 3 4. First test the effects of S1 and S2 separately and together prior to learning. Then input the pairing associating S1 + S2 with the response, and initiate learning. This should reach criterion very rapidly. Again test with S1 and S2 separately and together. You should now find that all combinations produce the correct response.

Restart by clicking *Options* and then *Clear Patterns*. Input the pairing associating S1 alone with the response. Initiate learning and let it run to criterion. Then without clearing the patterns or making any other change input the compound stimulus associating S1 + S2 with the response and initiate learning. Learning should again be fast, and testing will then show that both S1 and S1 + S2 produce the required response but that S2 alone does not.

Kamin blocking is most commonly interpreted by thinking of learning as the correcting of erroneous expectations. Prior learning that associates one stimulus with the response produces expectations that turn out to be correct when the compound stimulus trials are given, so no learning then occurs.

The application of this interpretation to the current results seems valid because the Delta rule corrects internally generated patterns of activation that do not match those that are externally specified. Error correction thus implies blocking. Blocking does not necessarily imply that an error correcting rule has been used, however. To see blocking without error correction repeat the exercise using the Hebbian pattern associator. If blocking effects imply the use of an error correcting rule then they should not occur when Hebbian rules are used. However you will find that the blocking shown in this exercise does occur when using some of the Hebbian rules.

Learning regularities and exceptions

In Program 3 we briefly discussed the need to learn regularities despite exceptions to them. You can explore this further here. We suggest a simplified version of the rule of 7 and 8 that McClelland and Rumelhart developed to illustrate this issue. We call it the rule of 5 and 6. It uses a net with 6 input units and 6 output units. Inputs and outputs have one, and only one, unit active from each of the pairs 1 and 2, 3 and 4, and 5 and 6. Thus there are always 3 units active in each pattern of 6 units. The mapping rule is that input units map into the same number output unit except for units 5 and 6, each of which is mapped into the other. An exception to this mapping rule is included; 2 4 6 maps into 2 4 6, rather than into 2 4 5 as specified by the rule.

With these specifications there are just 8 possible inputs. The file RULE6-6 (short for a mapping rule in a 6 into 6 unit net) contains 7 of them with the exception as the last item. One regular mapping, 2 3 5 into 2 3 6 has been omitted so that the generalisation of the rule to new inputs can be tested.

Select a 6 (input) into 6 (output) net, use a logistic output function, and set the learning rate to 1.0. Load the file RULE6-6 using *Filer In*, then click *Input* 6 times to load the first 6 input-output pairs which are all regular. Initiate learning by clicking *Learn*, and you will see that it reaches criterion in only about 18 epochs. A careful examination of the weights will show how they have incorporated the regularities. Testing will confirm that they have done so successfully.

Now add the seventh irregular pair by clicking *Input* once more, and then restart the learning by clicking *Learn*. It takes longer to reach criterion this time, needing about another 54 epochs to incorporate this one extra irregular item. Had it been regular then many fewer learning epochs would have been needed. Testing will confirm that although the exception has been learned the regular items are still remembered. More importantly the rule is also still remembered, and this can be tested by presenting the input that was omitted during training, i.e. 2 3 5.

It will be instructive to examine the weights to see how the trick is done. The irregular item is 2 4 6. The 2 and the 4 are mapped regularly but the 6 is not. What happens is that the context of the irregular mapping, the 2 and the 4, forms strong excitatory connections with the irregular part of the response, i.e. a 6 in the output rather than a 5. The connections from input units 1 and 4 to output unit 5 are strengthened to balance this out in other contexts. In the context of input units 2 and 4, therefore, but in no other, the irregular mapping wins out over the connections that embody the regularity.

Many variations on this exercise are possible. For example, what happens if the context of the exception is presented by itself at test? Does it matter whether the exception is learned before, after, or together with the regular items?

Another important issue concerns the ability of Hebbian rules to solve this problem. The file RULE6-6 can be used with Program 2 of this chapter to explore this issue. You are likely to find that none of those rules can learn both the rules and the exception fully, but that two of them come close, with the Pre-synaptic rule in particular doing very well.

Solving mappings where pair-wise correlations are inadequate

Hebbian learning rules are dominated by correlations or the conditional probabilities of activity between each of the individual pairings of input and output units. A classification problem that could not be solved by such relations was presented in the last exercise for the Hebbian pattern associators. This problem is in the data file HARD4-1, and can be used here with the Delta rule.

Select a 4 (input) into 1 (output) net, use a logistic output function, and set the learning rate to 1.0. Use *Filer In* to load HARD4-1, click *Input* 4 times, input HARD4-1, and then initiate learning by clicking *Learn*, and watch what happens. Basically, the result is that whereas the Hebbian rules cannot solve this mapping, the Delta rule can. Even for the Delta rule it is a hard problem, however. Even though it uses a smaller net and fewer pattern pairs than the rule of 5 and 6, it takes as long to solve.

Learning a bias to being "on" or "off"

In the previous exercise one input unit, unit 1, was on all the time. This unit therefore carried no information, and was thus in that sense redundant. This unit is not redundant in the sense that the problem can be solved by the Delta rule without it, however. You can confirm this by repeating that exercise, using direct mouse input, except omitting unit 1.

The reason for the anomaly is that the Delta rule can use an input unit that is on all the time to bias an output unit to being either on or off. To see how this can be useful consider the case where we want an output unit to come on when both of two input units are on but not when just one of them is. This can be achieved by giving the unit a bias to being off that can be overcome by two positive inputs, but not by either alone. Without such a bias then each positive input alone would tend to produce a positive output.

Use a 3 (input) into 2 (output) net. Input unit 1 will be a bias unit so it will be on in all inputs. Input the three pairs (1 2 3 into 1; 1 2 into 2; 1 3 into 2), and then initiate learning. In this case learning will be fastest using a linear output function with a learning rate of 0.6.

The resulting weight matrix is simple and informative. One output unit uses the weight from the bias unit to learn a bias to being off, and the other output unit uses it to learn a bias to being on.

Repetition of this exercise using the Hebbian rules will also be instructive.

What nets with a single layer of weights cannot learn

Nets with units whose activations are just the sum of their weighted inputs and with only a single layer of weights cannot learn to respond to relations between the different inputs. The most used example of this is the problem of the exclusive-or. Imagine that there are two lights which may be either on or off. We want a response if one of the lights is on. We don't want a response if both lights are on, or if neither light is on.

This task can be studied using a 3 (input) into 2 (output) net as in the last exercise, and by adding just one further input pair. Input the four pairs (1 2 3 into 1; 1 2 into 2; 1 3 into 2; 1 into 1), and then initiate learning. You will find that this problem cannot be solved, no matter which output function you use, nor how you set the learning rate.

Remember that you can click the mouse button to interrupt learning. Otherwise it will just go on indefinitely.

Problems of this kind have gained such prominence not only because single-layer nets cannot learn them but because multi-layer nets can. The following chapter on backpropagation shows how.

Suggestions for further reading

There is much relevant material in the two volumes on Parallel Distributed Processing by McClelland and Rumelhart (1986). See Chapters 1, 2, and 3 for an introduction, and Chapters 18 and 19 for cognitive applications.

Anderson (1983) gives an introduction that emphasises Hebbian rules, neurobiology, and cognition. A more advanced and recent analysis of Hebbian rules in a pattern associator is provided by Willshaw and Dayan (1990). Rumelhart and McClelland's account of past tense learning is in Volume 2, Chapter 18, of Parallel Distributed Processing (1986). A lengthy critique is offered by Pinker and Prince (1988), and a shorter, more digestible summary of their argument is in Prince and Pinker (1988).

Kamin Blocking and other associative learning phenomena are discussed in relation to PDP and neural nets in McLaren, Kaye and Mackintosh (1989), and in Sutton and Barto (1981).

7

Backpropagation

Single-layer pattern associators can have powerful computational properties as the "Rule of 7 and 8" and Rumelhart and McClelland's past-tense learning demonstrate. There are limitations however to the associations that can be represented in a single-layer net. The nets are "good" at mapping between input and output patterns that are similar, but if the structural similarity between input and output patterns is poor then the net may be unable to perform the mapping i.e., there are some pattern pairs that the net cannot recognise no matter how much learning takes place.

There is a developmental history for neural networks as in any science and much of this has revolved around the capabilities of single-layer nets, or, to put it another way, an evaluation of the usefulness of nets which lack the capacity for internal representation. The prominent figures in a lengthy debate over several decades were Frank Rosenblatt (e.g., Rosenblatt, 1962) who invented simple neural nets based on "Perceptrons", claiming that these processing units were capable of mapping any association between any input and output pattern sets, and Marvin Minsky and Seymour Papert (Cf., Minsky and Papert, 1969) who formally proved that these single-layer processing systems were severely limited and could not live up to Rosenblatt's claims. The history and importance of this issue is discussed in various parts of the PDP books, particularly in the introductions to Chapters 5 and 8.

Some of the limitations of pattern associators with a single layer of weights were outlined in the previous chapter and the present chapter looks at one solution to these limitations.

Multi-layer nets with hidden units can learn internal representations which mediate between input and output. The possible advantages of hidden units was realised by both Rosenblatt and by Minsky and Papert, but it was only recently that an effective learning algorithm for training such system was devised. This is "backpropagation", the commonly used short form of "backpropagation of the Delta rule". It is described by Rumelhart, Hinton and Williams (1986) and is a modification and extension of the Delta rule that you have encountered in earlier modules. In brief, backpropagation works as follows: The network is presented with pairs of input and target patterns. The output for each unit in the net is calculated by computing the product of the inputs multiplied by the weights at connections between the inputs and output unit. If there is no difference between the actual output and the target output required then no learning takes place. When there is a difference then the weights connecting the various layers are adjusted to produce the required target output.

Although backpropagation has been applied to a wide variety of architectures, the present module illustrates one of the simpler forms of multi-layer systems, a fully-connected feed-forward network. A layered feed-forward net can have any number of layers of hidden units. This module, in common with many investigations in the literature, examines three-layer nets with one hidden layer, one input layer and one output layer. Hidden units (sometimes called intermediate units) are so-called because they neither receive input from, nor send outputs to, units outside the net. Output units cannot receive signals directly from the input layer. Activation flows in only one direction, from input to output through the hidden units. The architecture of the net is more easily comprehended diagrammatically in Figure 7.1 which is a representation of a three-layer net commonly found in the literature. It has the advantage that the layering and feedforward process is clear at a glance, but the disadvantage that the display of weights at connections between units is unclear and clumsy. Weights can be more adequately displayed using the graphical representation shown in Figure 7.2 which is similar to the representations displayed in the programs.

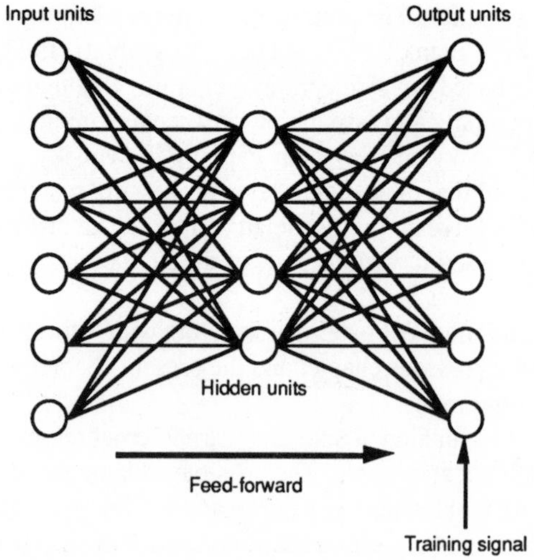

Figure 7.1. A common representation of a three-layer feed-forward net with 6 input units, 4 hidden units and 6 output units

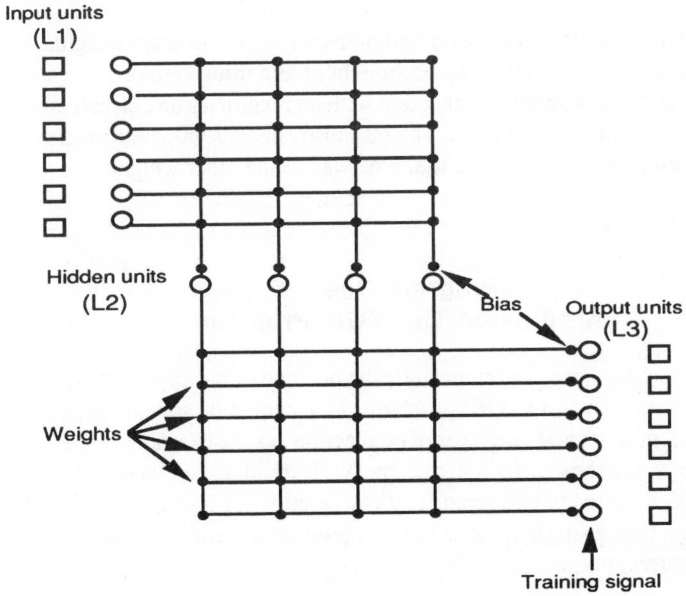

Figure 7.2. Schematic representation of a 6 input, 4 hidden, 6 output net similar to those used in the program simulations

Activation function

Output and hidden units both use a logistic activation function similar to the one you have already encountered in the Delta pattern associators. Each unit computes a net input by summing the value of the inputs multiplied by the weights on its connections (i.e., by summing the weighted inputs). The backpropagation learning rule requires a continuous, nonlinear activation function between 0 and 1. The net input to each unit is "squashed" between 0 and 1 but never quite reaches those values. Figure 7.3 illustrates the activation function. (For further details see Appendix 3)

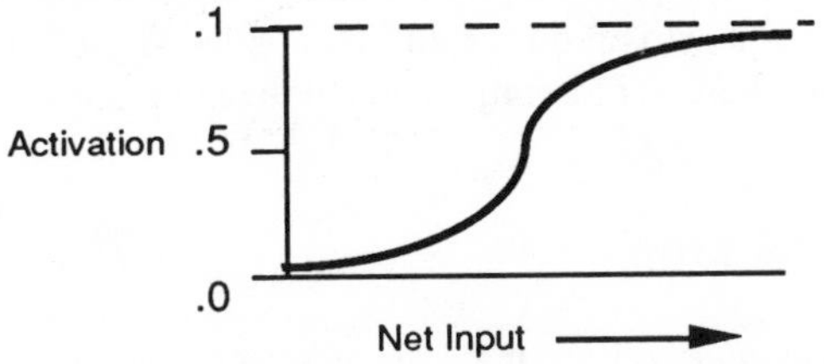

Fig 7.3. The S-shaped logistic function which derives a continuous, nonlinear activation from the net input to the unit

Bias

Note that each unit of the hidden layer and output layer has an extra weight. This is often called the bias and may be thought of as a threshold, or alternatively, as the weight on a connection with an imaginary unit which is always on (i.e., having a value of 1). The bias also changes value during the course of learning and is updated in the same way as the other weights.

Program One
Introduction:The XOR Problem

One of the classic exercises to demonstrate the power of a backpropagated three layer net is the exclusive-or (XOR) problem which cannot be solved using nets with two layers of units and one layer of connections as the example in the previous chapter has shown. To reiterate; the XOR problem can be stated in the following way. If there are two inputs that can be either or both on or off, and one output unit, then a single-layer net cannot produce a weights matrix which will give the correct output for the following:

If neither unit is on then output =0
If both units are on then output =0
If either unit is on then output =1

The exclusive-or problem then is "either one or the other but not both".
The XOR is demonstrated in a three-layer net with a set of four patterns of two inputs and target output.

Input	Output
0 0	0
1 1	0
1 0	1
0 1	1

The two patterns which differ most (11 and 00) have to produce the same output (0) within a context where the two other patterns (01 and 10), which overlap with both of these, have to produce a different output (1). The hidden layer allows for a representation of a conjunction of the input units.

How to use the program

Select *Backpropagation* from the main menu, select *Introduction: The XOR problem*. The program operates either as a demonstration of the problem and its solution,or as an illustration of how learning takes place in backpropagation.

Demonstration mode

Select *Continue.* on the program's title page. The 2 (input), 2 (hidden), 1 (output) three-layer net is presented. Select *Input* and click the mouse button four times to input the pattern set. Ensure that the learning rate (select *Learning*) is set to 0.3 and the momentum term (select *Momentum*) to 0.85. Select *Learn* and the net will commence learning the pattern set. The sum squared error for each pattern pair is displayed above the Output units. If you move the mouse laterally across the patterns you can obtain the error readout for all pattern pairs in the set. The learning procedure will cease when the error for each pattern pair is less than or equal to 0.1 when the *Error* display disappears. Select *Test* then *Verify* to ensure that the net has learned the patterns.

Try running the XOR problem on a few different trials (select *Options* then *Clear Weights*), with various learning rates and momentum values. You may notice that although the outcome might be the same the solution is sometimes different, i.e., different combinations of excitatory and inhibitory weight values can produce the same result. Different solutions arise because the weights are initialised to small random excitatory and inhibitory values at the start of each new trial, producing a different error value for the same input-target pairs.

Rumelhart and colleagues (1986) have found that the learning rate is extremely important for reliable solution of the XOR problem. With learning rates above 0.75 the procedure tends to become unstable and gets stuck whereas learning rates at 0.1 and below require a high number of epochs to solution. They found acceptable performance with a learning rate around 0.25

If you use a high learning rate you may find that on some occasions the net may not solve the problem and appears to be "stuck" with each input-target pair showing an unchanging error across a number of epochs. What has probably happened is that the learning procedure has become stuck in a local minima in the gradient descent procedure. What do these terms "gradient descent" and "local minima" mean?

Gradient descent and local minima

Gradient descent means that the error is always changing in a downward direction. Sometimes this leads to a situation where gradient descent gets stuck in local mimina. Hinton and Sejnowski's (1986) ball-bearing analogy is a good way of comprehending this concept. Figure 7.4 shows the profile of a landscape (an error landscape). A ball-bearing released on the top right-hand side of the landscape will always travel downhill towards the lowermost point (B) which we can think of as the lowermost energy point or minimum error. If the ball-bearing gets trapped at the local minima point (A) it gets stuck because it cannot go uphill against gravity. In an analogous way the error in backpropagation cannot increase, so the weights settle on values which minimise the error at that point (local minima), precluding a satisfactory solution. One way of reducing the likelihood that gradient descent will get stuck in small local minima is to introduce a momentum term.

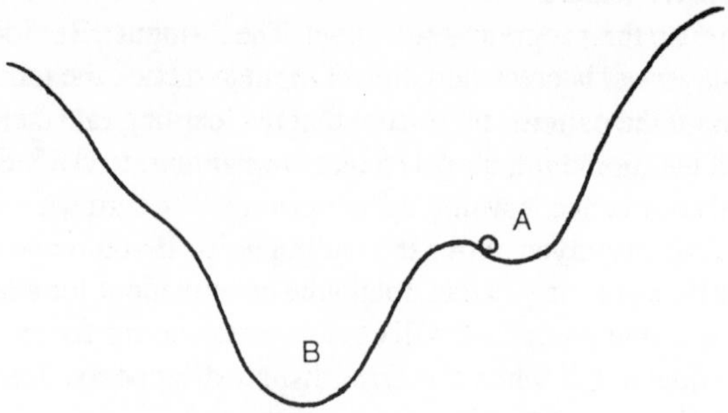

Figure 7.4. A landscape profile representing local minima in the gradient descent procedure. The ball-bearing can become stuck at A because it is unable to move the small uphill distance to reach the lowermost point B

Momentum

Ideally we want any problem to be solved as quickly as possible. We know that within limits the higher the learning rate the fewer number of epochs are required. However the gradient descent procedure employed requires that the learning rate is set low enough to avoid oscillation, i.e., avoid a situation where the weight change is so great that it "bounces" back and forward between positive and negative values without ever arriving at a satisfactory solution. The momentum term is a modification of the basic backpropagation procedure and allows a higher learning rate while keeping the risk of oscillation to a minimum. The momentum parameter is a constant which determines the direction of movement in error space, based on the effect of past weight changes. Oscillation can still be found in attempted solutions to the XOR problem, particularly when the learning rate is set very high (e.g., 0.95). You can probably produce oscillations if you wish by setting *Momentum* = 0 and *Learning* = 1.

Backpropagation can solve the XOR with no momentum if the learning rate is set low. To demonstrate this set Momentum = 0 and Learning = 0.1.

Tutorial mode: Learning in Backpropagation

Select *Tutorial.* Click on *Continue* for each of the steps below which are illustrated diagrammatically on the screen. The program will continue through the sequence until you press the middle button on the mouse to exit.

Note: This section is designed primarily for beginners or readers who require only a broad conceptual understanding of backpropagation. There is a more detailed explanation of the procedure in Appendix 3.

The objective for the procedure is to learn a set of weights which will provide the correct output for each each input in the pattern set of input-target pairs. For clarity let us consider the procedure for just one of the pattern pairs.

Learning takes place in two principle stages, a forward pass to compute activation levels and a backward pass to calculate the error terms and adjust the weights, with several steps in each stage. The weights are initially set to small positive and negative random values prior to learning. Note that the activation and output of each unit are treated as the same value in the following text, so that if we refer to "the output of Unit X" this is equivalent to "the activation of Unit X".

Forward pass to compute activation and output

1. The net input for each hidden unit (L2) is calculated by multiplying the inputs (L1) by the weights on connections between the inputs and the hidden unit.
2. The activation for each hidden unit is a function of the net input from L1, calculated using a sigmoid (S-shaped) logistic function which produces an output between 0 and 1 (see Figure 7.3).
3. The net input for the output unit (L3) is calculated by multiplying the activations of the hidden layer (L2) by the weights on connections between L2 and L3.
4. The activation for each output unit is a function of the net input from L2, and is calculated using the same logistic function as the hidden units.

Backward pass to calculate the error and update the weights

1. The difference between the activation of the L3 output unit and the required target output is calculated.
2. The error signal (Delta) from the output unit is the derivative of this difference. Don't worry if you are unfamiliar with derivatives because it is not essential to a conceptual understanding of what is going on. Remember that the logistic activation function produces activations between 0 and 1. When the activation is in its midrange, say 0.5, the derivative produces a large error signal. As the activation approaches 0 or 1 the derivative (i.e., the error signal) reduces towards zero. This has the neat effect of making large changes to the weights when the output unit is neither fully on or off (i.e., it is "uncommitted") and smaller "fine-tuning" of the weights as the output unit approaches its correct value (i.e., when actual output = target output).
3. Now change the weights between L2 and L3. The weight change at each connection between L2 and L3 is calculated using a proportion (the learning rate) of the error term from the L3 output unit, the current value of the weight, the output of each hidden layer unit in L2, and the momentum factor. Each weight is then updated by adding the weight change to the old weight value.
4. The next step is to calculate the effect of the error produced in the hidden units (L2) on the error at the output unit (L3). Remember that the activation for

each hidden unit was calculated in the forward pass. The derivative of the activation of each hidden unit is calculated and then an error term is computed. The error term is the product of the derivative and the error produced by the output unit (L3) multiplied by the weights between L2 and L3.
5. Now change the weights between L1 and L2. The weight change at each connection between L1 and L2 is calculated using a proportion (the learning rate) of the error produced at L2, the current value of the weight, and the value of the input unit to which it is connected. Each weight is then updated by adding the weight change to the old weight value (Easy isn't it?!).

The error and consequent weight changes are computed for each pattern in the pattern set. The amount of the weight change, determined by the learning rate parameter, is normally a small proportion of the error, so that the weights are changed slightly for each pattern, then the cycle starts again until the total error for each pattern is acceptably near zero (e.g., 0.1).

This procedure for adjusting weights after each pattern is sometimes termed "on-line", in contrast with an alternative procedure ("off-line", not used in the present programs) which adjusts the weights only after the error for all the pattern pairs has been calculated at the end of each epoch.

Program Two: Build your own Backpropagation net

How to use the program

Select *Backpropagation* from the main menu, then *Build your own Backprop Net.* Select the number of units you require for each layer of the net. The net will be automatically displayed with vertical input units to the left, horizontal hidden units in the centre and vertical output units to the right.

The value of the learning rate and momentum parameters can be set by clicking *Learning* or *Momentum.* These parameters can be changed at any time during program use. To change parameters while the program is cycling through its learning stage click the mouse button, change parameters, then return to learning by clicking *Learn.* The learning cycle will continue from the interrupt.

A pattern set to be learned can be input directly using the mouse, can be generated at random, or can be input from file. To generate new patterns at random click *Random,* and specify the proportion of units to be active, before clicking *Input.* Each click on *Input* will then bring in a new random pattern. To bring in a file of patterns to be learned click *Filer In* and then type the file name on the keyboard, in CAPITALS, ending with a return. Each click on *Input* will then bring in the next pattern from the file. If you wish to cancel the *Random* or *File In* functions, select *Options* then either *Reset Weights* or *Clear Patterns.*

To learn the set of patterns that you have input click *Learn.* The backpropagation procedure commences immediately. The error and unit activation levels are displayed for pattern 1 in the pattern set. Unit activation levels are open circles which "fill" with activation as usual, and the total error for the pattern is shown in the rectangle above the output units. The error and activation levels for the other patterns can be displayed by moving the pointer along the pattern set. Remember that the sum error displayed is the sum squared difference between the output produced by the net and the output specified by the training signal. The learning cycle terminates when the total error for each of the patterns is less than or equal to 0.1, or it can be terminated voluntarily by clicking the mouse button.

To save a pattern set for later use click *Filer Out*, and specify the file name on the keyboard, in CAPITALS,and press <Return>.

To present patterns for test click *Test*. You will then be asked whether you wish to *Verify*? If you wish to specify test inputs using the mouse click *No*. If you wish to present just the learned patterns for test click *Yes*, then specify the strength of these test input patterns. The net will then be presented with whichever learned input the mouse pointer is aimed at.

Exercises

All the exercises suggested for the Hebbian and Delta pattern associators can be repeated using backpropagation. In particular, you should try the tasks that could not be solved by the Delta rule in a simple feed-forward net without hidden layers.

Determining the size of hidden layers

One common problem using nets with hidden layers is how to decide the size of the hidden layer. This exercise gives some insight into the problem by posing a pattern set and comparing performance across nets with different numbers of hidden units. If you run the simulation several times for each sized hidden layer you will probably note different outcomes for each size. This is due partly to differences in the initial random weights on connections prior to learning. Select an 8 (input) 4 (hidden) 8 (output) net and input the following two pattern pairs:

	Input	Output
Pattern A	1 3 5 7	1 4 6 8
Pattern B	2 4 5 8	2 3 6 7

Select *Learning* of 0.9 and *Momentum* of 0.8. Select *Learn* and the net should learn within 20 cycles. Select *Test* then *Verify* that the net has learned the pairings. Select *Test* then *Verify-No* to test for generalisation using part of the input patterns. You will probably find that this is not always perfect and the output often surprising. For example, Test patterns 6 8 and 2 3, often show peculiar output while test pattern 6 7 gives a more-or-less predictable output. Run the simulation a few times and note different weight assignment on each occasion, and the consequences of this for pattern generalisation. Repeat the exercise with different numbers of hidden units.

Question: What are the minimum and maximum number of units in the hidden layer for reliable solution of this problem? What happens between these two extremes?

Parity

The parity problem, discussed by Minsky & Papert (1969), and more recently by Rumelhart et al (1986), shows how a net with hidden units can learn to provide an active response when the input has an odd number of active units and not respond when the input pattern has an even number of units. Nets with only a single layer of weights are unable to perform this apparently simple operation because closer examination of the problem reveals that it is in fact very difficult. The most similar patterns, differing by only a single unit (e.g., 3 active units = output of 1; 4 active units = output of 0), have to provide a completely different output. Conversely, patterns differing by a large number of inputs have to provide the same output

Select a 4 (input), 4 (hidden), 1 (output) net. Select *Filer In*, type PARITY and press <Return>. Click on *Input* five times for the following pattern pairs;.

Input pattern	Output pattern
0 0 0 0	0
1 0 0 0	1
1 1 0 0	0
1 1 1 0	1
1 1 1 1	0

Select *Learn*. The net should learn the mapping within about 20 cycles. Select *Test* and *Verify* that the net produces the correct input-output mappings. If you clear the weights (select *Options*, then *Clear Weights*) and then learn the pattern set again you may notice that different hidden units become active for each of the pattern pairs. You may also notice that the number of hidden units that become active for each input pattern depends on the number of "off" (0) units in that pattern. The internal representation is encoding only the number of zeros, the identity of the active units is not represented.

The encoder problem

The encoder problem might seem a little odd on first encounter but it reveals one striking property of a three-layer backpropagation net. The problem is simply to map the input into the output when the hidden layer contains only a small number of units (e.g., equal to the log of the number of input or output units).

This small number of hidden units has to encode the the set of input patterns and then decode the output of the hidden units back into the same pattern set for the output units.

This exercise demonstrates the encoder problem with a net of eight input and output units and three (log 8) hidden units. Restart the program (select *Options* then *Restart Program*) if you are already working on it and select an 8 (input), 3 (hidden), 8 (output) net. Set *Learning* to 0.3 and *Momentum* to 0.85. Select *Filer In*, type in the filename ENCODE and press <Return>. Input all of the eight patterns by clicking on *Input*. Note that all patterns are orthogonal with only one active unit in each input or output pattern. Select Learn and then sit back. Learning usually takes place within 700-1000 epochs and will cease when the error on all the input-target pairs is less than or equal to 0.1. Select *Test* and *Verify* that the pattern set has been learned.

It might seem unlikely *a priori* that the hidden units are capable of encoding the input pattern set and then decoding the same patterns again for output, yet the procedure can achieve this and is capable of learning quite different internal representations across a number of trials. If you test the net (Select *Test*, then *Verify-No* you will find that the encoding is highly resistant to noisy input. A suitable test is to provide a test input of 1 to any unit and noise in the form of small (0.1 to 0.3) inputs to the other units. The net (usually reliably) gives an active output corresponding to the active input and zero output to the noise.

Further exercises

Rumelhart, Hinton and Williams (1986, pp 345-348) show how nets with hidden layers can code for symmetry in patterns and perform binary addition. The interested reader is advised to follow up these and other exercises in that reference.

Discussion

Backpropagation in its various forms is probably the most powerful learning algorithm commonly cited in the literature and there is little doubt that its discovery has given great impetus to work in connectionism and neural computation. The paradigm does however suffer a few problems, two of which are the ability to generalise and biological plausibility.

Generalisation. You may have noticed that for some pattern sets (e.g., the XOR), that test performance using weaker (<1) inputs of the original pattern set (e.g., *Verify* with *Strength* = 0.4) gives an unreliable output. This is very different from our own ability for recognizing patterns with a low signal strength.

The ability to generalise in other ways is fundamental to learning in humans and other higher animals. We must have an ability to generalise learning of important attributes from one situation to another. For example, infants learn to generalise from one or two examples of faces (their parents) to recognition of faces as a general category of things in the world, even though faces are well known to change quite dramatically by individual, expression and viewpoint. Backpropagated nets do contain the ability to generalise quite sensibly, but they can lose this ability as learning improves, especially for "easy" mappings where the are plenty of hidden units. If a particular net is trained on a set of example input-output pairs it can usually generalise the learning to produce an appropriate output to similar previously unseen test examples. The problem occurs when the net's ability to generalise decreases across a number of training epochs, as shown in Figure 7.5. Performance on the test examples improves linearly with the training epochs until a plateau is reached. After this point test performance gets markedly worse until generalisation is unreliable. What happens is that the net "overlearns" and starts adapting the weights to encode individual pattern pairs, thereby losing its capacity to map the training set more globally, resulting in loss of generalisation.

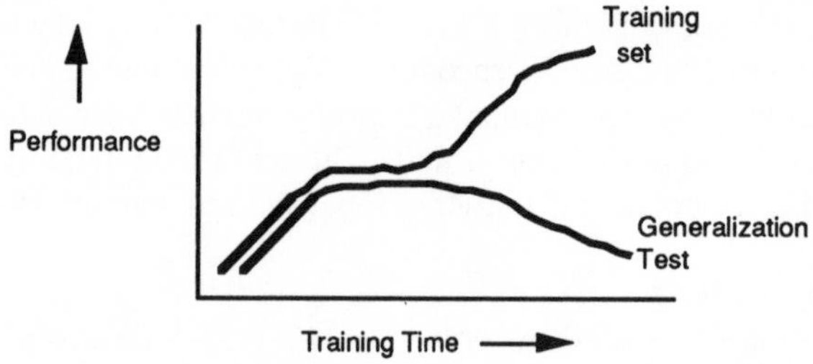

Figure 7.5. Generalisation performance on test trails increases linearly with training time until the net "overlearns" the training set, thereafter test performance can deteriorate sharply (from Knight 1989, p16)

Biological plausibility. Back propagation is a powerful connectionist model based loosely on neuron-like units, but is it a truly *neural* computation model, i.e., is there any evidence for such a learning architecture in the brain? The current answers to this question are;

1. No, there is no evidence for similar multi-layer error correcting architectures in the brain.
2. Even if there were similar nets it is difficult to see how input units could receive appropriate teaching/training signals.
3. Backpropagation usually takes hundreds of training epochs to learn even a modest set of input-target pairs. This is quite unlike human or animal learning which commonly takes place with far fewer presentations.

None of these problems are fatal because the benefit of backpropagation is that it shows how internal representations might mediate the required information from input to output. This has led many researchers to look for alternative, more biologically plausible, learning procedures which show the same strengths and capabilities of backpropagation but which are more firmly linked to viable neural architecture.

Further reading

"Learning Internal Representations by Error Propagation" by Rumelhart, Hinton and Williams in PDP Volume 1 (Chapter 8) is the original and principle source for further reading on backpropagation. The relationship between PDP models (including backpropagation), cognitive science and neuroscience is discussed in Part IV of PDP Volume 2.

In "Modelling Cortical Computation with Backpropagation" Zipser (1990) discusses the role of the teaching input in identity mapping (a variation on backpropagation where the input is also the training signal).

8

Competitive Learning

Competitive learning nets are layered self-organizing systems that consist of excitatory connections between layers and competition between units within layers. They can have any number of layers. A major difference between these nets and pattern associators is that these do not need a supervisor during learning to tell the net what output it should be producing, i.e., the learning is unsupervised. The net is not taught to pair input patterns with externally specified output patterns but learns how to use the output activity to discriminate as well as possible between different instances of the input patterns that it actually receives. As the number of different output patterns that the net can produce is usually very much less than the number of input patterns that it can receive it has to maximise discrimination by finding useful summary statistics. For example, one useful summary statistic of some measure that varies from instance to instance is whether it is greater or less than its average value across many instances. Suppose that you need to say something about a person's height but have only one bit of information to do it. One obviously good way to use that bit would be to say short or tall. Or suppose that you wish to say something about a persons appearance again using only one bit. It is far less obvious how to use the bit in this case but there are many possibilities. For example you could use the bit to say male or female, or young or old. If you had two bits one could be used for sex and the other for age. That would probably be more informative than using both bits to specify one of the variables more precisely.

The basic role of competitive nets is therefore to find summary statistics that convey much less information than the input data as a whole but that still discriminates between different instances well. The ability to do this will be particularly useful when there is a high degree of structure in the input. Put most simply what we mean by structure is that the regions of input space within which the inputs actually occur are much less than that space as a whole, i.e. the variety of input patterns that actually occurs is much less than could possibly occur. For example, height can be used because people have a long axis. If we were some alien species that had very complex shapes with many spiky bits that poked out in different directions at different times and no long axes or axes of symmetry it would not be of much use to try and measure height.

The dimensions of variation that are useful therefore depends upon what does and does not vary in the population. The beauty of competitive nets is that they can discover these dimensions for themselves.

Competitive nets can also be designed to have another basic capability. This is concerned with similarity, continuity, or neighbourliness. Nets can be designed so that inputs that are similar or near to each other in the input space are represented by outputs that are similar or near each other in the output space. These are valuable abilities. For example, the auto-associative nets and pattern matching nets that we discussed in Chapter 5 and 6 automatically tend to treat similar patterns in similar ways. Such generalisation will be appropriate if the represention that are input to these nets have been discovered by appropriately designed competitive nets because then similar inputs will be represented in similar ways.

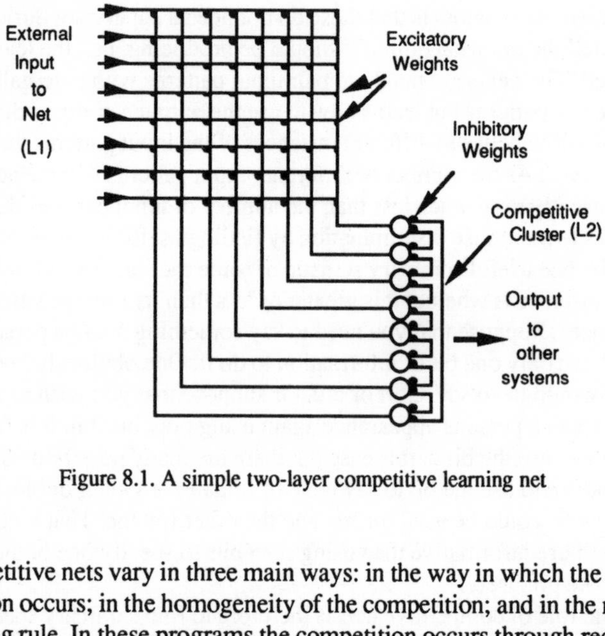

Figure 8.1. A simple two-layer competitive learning net

Competitive nets vary in three main ways: in the way in which the competition occurs; in the homogeneity of the competition; and in the nature of the learning rule. In these programs the competition occurs through reciprocal inhibition between output units. This is a common and biologically plausible procedure. The architecture of a simple two-layer competitive learning net of this kind is shown in Figure 8.1. The lowest layer (L1) is the input layer, and the next (L2) is the output layer (also called the competitive cluster). Each unit in L1 sends excitatory inputs to each unit in L2, through weights that are initially set at random. Units within L2 reciprocally inhibit each other. They therefore compete so that those most strongly activated by the input reduce the activity of those less strongly activated. If every L2 unit inhibits every other equally strongly then the competition is homogeneous. It is also possible to put structure into the inhibition. For example, each unit may inhibit only its neighbour as emphasized in Figure 8.2. In that case it would be described as lateral inhibition as in Chapter 4. Note that in Figure 8.2. the lateral inhibition is with 'wrap-round', i.e. units at each end inhibit each other.

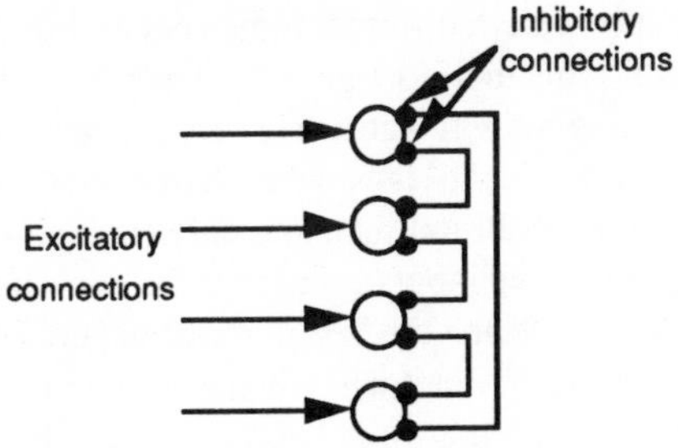

Figure 8.2. A four unit inhibitory cluster

The different learning rules are all variants on the theme of moving the input weight vector of the currently successful output unit or units towards the current input vector. The two used in these programs are the Stent-Singer rule, and the Rumelhart and Zipser rule. Both change only the weights of successful units. The Stent-Singer rule is just as used in Chapters 5 and 6. The Rumelhart and Zipser rule normalises the total value of the weights coming into each unit from L1. That is it ensures that the sum of its positive L2 input weights is always 1. In effect it increases the weights to the unit on those input lines that are currently active, and then decreases all weights so that their sum still equals one. Both rules move the part of the input field to which the unit responds towards the currently active input units and away from the currently silent input units.

To understand the way that these nets work imagine the L2 units as having receptive fields within the input space. These are specified by their input weights. For example, in Figure 8.1. the receptive field of the output unit nearest the top of the figure is specified by the column of weights at the far right of the weights matrix. If that unit were to be successful in the competition resulting from some particular input pattern then its weights would be changed so that it would respond even more strongly to that input pattern in future and less strongly to other patterns. Put simply its input weights would be changed to more closely fit the current input. As there are 8 input units in Figure 8.1 any input and any column of weights can be thought of as a points or vectors in 8-dimensional space. The learning rule can then be thought of as moving the weight vector towards the input vector by an amount determined by a learning rate parameter.

To understand the dynamics of the learning process first imagine a net with only one output unit and the learning rate set so that the weight vector moved all the way to the input vector. All that would then happen is that the weight vector would simply jump around with the inputs and nothing would be learned. However, if the learning rate is made small there will be an important difference. The weight vector will then move gradually towards the centre of the set of input patterns and then stay near it. Note that the average value of the weight vector will not depend just upon which different inputs occur, but also upon how often they occur. The learning rule therefore pulls the weight vectors towards inputs that actually do occur, and more towards those that occur more often.

Now to understand the effect of the competitive interactions imagine a net with two output units and inhibition such that only one unit is successful at any one time. Also imagine that the inputs occur in some particular sub-sections of the whole input space only. When the first instance occurs whichever unit has its weight vector closest to that input will win the competition and move towards that input, and thus away from the weight vector of the other unit, which will itself not move in this instance. When an input occurs that is closer to the weight vector of the second unit it will move towards that input and away from the weight vector of the first unit.

The learning rule therefore moves the weight vectors towards regions were instances occur, and the competition spreads them out. Thus the final result is usually that the complete set of weight vectors will be within the regions of input space where inputs actually occur, and well spread out within that space.

The programs and exercises that follow are designed to illustrate and develop these points, and to allow you to discover further properties and capabilities of these nets for yourself.

Learning rules

The two learning procedures presented in this module are based on the Stent-Singer rule and Rumelhart and Zipser's normalisation procedure. For both rules learning takes place through modification of the weights at connections between L1 and L2. The only weights modified are those on connections between the active unit (or units) in L2 and related inputs in L1.

The Stent-Singer rule is the same as for auto-association and pattern association. Weights on connections with active input units are increased. Weights on connections with inactive input units are decreased.

Rumelhart and Zipser's normalisation procedure stipulates that the sum of the weights between the input units and each output unit has to be kept equal to 1. In order to achieve this, all the weights in the connections between the active unit(s) in L2 and the input units in L1 are decreased by a small amount.

The only weights increased are those between the active unit(s) in L2 and the active units in L1. The amount of the increase is determined such that the total weight on connections to each output unit is again equal to 1

Program One: Introduction

One important characteristic of competitive learning nets is their ability to reduce the information presented in a set of input patterns to a relatively few output units which retain a coding of the structure that is in the input pattern. It can be argued (e.g., by Kohonen, 1984) that the ability to reduce the information present in a set of visuo-spatial patterns by compressing it into a simplified representation which retains the spatial relationships between the patterns is an essential characteristic of information processing in the brain. Another way of stating this is to say that at some level of processing the relationship between sensory input patterns is more important than what the patterns themselves represent.

In the following competitive learning simulation twelve patterns are presented to a small net which has an input layer of nine units (L1) and an inhibitory cluster of three output units (L2). The input patterns could be the output from other nets, represent input from instrumentation, or represent a patch of light moving down a vertical slit (Figure 8.3). What we want is for the net to find a way of mapping these twelve patterns of nine units into only three outputs i.e., find a way of assigning the input patterns to 3 categories. The classification should preserve information on the structure in the input set.

The learning procedure for the net is as follows:

Each unit in L2 receives excitatory input from all the active units in L1. The activation level of each unit in L2 corresponds to the sum of its inputs multiplied by the weights.

Each unit in L2 also receives inhibitory inputs from adjacent (lateral) units in L2, equal to a proportion of their activation levels.

The competitive part of the process is where activation cycles within the inhibitory cluster a number of times until one unit or several units become highly activated. The only weights modified are those on connections between the active unit(s) in L2 and related inputs in L1.

This program uses the Stent-Singer learning rule to modify the weights.

Interpretation of the weight matrices

Each column can be seen as the receptive field of the output unit to which it is connected. Note that initially, prior to learning, some output units may have strong weights connecting them to input lines that are not contiguous (i.e., not adjacent). During learning the receptive field can be seen to change. The change is to adapt the receptive field to some part of the input net. For example, the receptive field becomes a contiguous area because that is how the patterns are structured in these input nets.

Different output units will usually have different receptive fields. This is due to the inhibition between the output units. The stronger the inhibition the less likely the receptive fields are to overlap. With weak inhibition they may overlap to some extent.

How to use the program

Select *Competitive Learning* from the main menu, then select *Introduction*. Select *Continue* after the title appears and a nine (input), three (competitive cluster) net will be displayed. Excitatory connections are shown as filled circles, inhibitory connections as lines connecting the output layer.

Select *Learn* from the control panel at the top of the screen. The program will complete learning phases shown as *Epochs* (one epoch = 10 activation cycles within the inhibitory cluster for each of the 12 patterns). You can interrupt learning to change parameters by clicking the button on the mouse. Once you have modified the relevant parameters select *Learn* and the program will continue.

Notice the pattern of excitatory connections between L1 and L2 and the way in which the net has organised the set of input patterns.

Testing the net

Select *Test* and check the net's performance by inputting any of the patterns. Choose a pattern (e.g. pattern 5), input one active unit from that pattern, and click the mouse button. Note the output pattern.

Click on *Continue* and repeat this using a different active unit from the same pattern until you have explored the whole pattern, noting the output for each input. You may notice that there is output for some units and not others.

Modifying net parameters

The net parameters can be adjusted, but they can have a complex interdependence which makes the outcome of multiple parameter changes difficult to predict. If the net has not classified the entire set of input patterns change a parameter, click *Learn* again and run the net for another 10 epochs.
Inhibit: The inhibition level alters the (non-adapting) inhibition between the units in the competitive cluster. When it is low, the cluster settles very slowly and there may be more than one active unit in the cluster. If this is the case then you may need to increase the inhibition parameter slightly.
Excite: The excitation level alters the amount of input from each input unit. If one pattern is not represented at all then increase excitation.
Output fn: The output function is a threshold below which the unit does not output to other units.

Exercises

The default values should be retained in the following exercises unless otherwise stated.

Repeat trials

There is no guarantee that the system will self-organise in the same way on different occasions because the weights are randomised prior to learning. It is worthwhile observing how the net classifies the output over a few trials (see Figure 8.3). To make this easier the initial weights for the program can be reset. Select *Options* then select *Reset Weights*, then select *Learn* to relearn and allow the net to self-organise again.

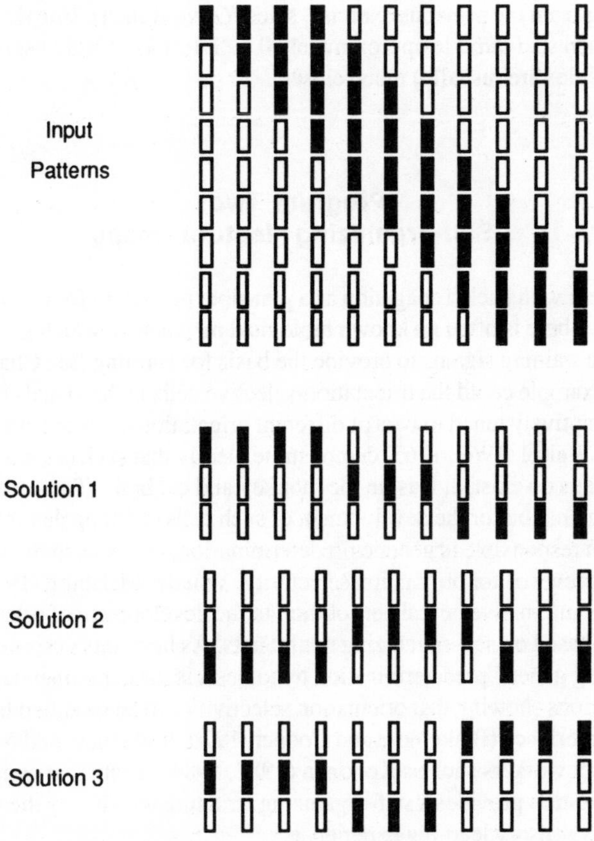

Figure 8.3. Three classifications of the input pattern. Note that for each classification a spatial relationship between patterns is retained in the coding.

Effects of the relative amounts of weight increase and decrease

There are two separate influences in the receptive field, one varies the width of the receptive field (ratio of weight increase to weight decrease) and the other varies the difference between the fields (the inhibition parameter).

For a constant amount of weight increase the receptive field gets narrower as the weight decrease gets larger. Therefore, the relative amounts of weight increase and weight decrease affect the width of the receptive fields. To see this run the simulation at default values. Note the width of the receptive fields (number of contiguous large weights). Select *Options*, then *Clear Weights.* set *Wt Dec* to 0.1. Select *Learn* and repeat previous test. Note now that the receptive fields are much narrower.

Effect of level of inhibition

Continuing from the previous exercise, select *Options* then *Clear Weights.* Click continue then set *Inhibit* to approximately 0.1. Select learn and observe that the receptive fields are (usually) much closer.

Program Two: Self-organizing feature maps

One problem with backpropagation as a plausible procedure for learning in the brain is that there is often no known biological mechanism which provides appropriate training signals to provide the basis for learning (see Chapter 7). How, for example could the orientation-selective cells in the visual cortex become adaptively tuned to bars of different orientations? Experiments by Hubel and Weisel (1962, 1963) demonstrate clearly that such orientation-sensitive cells do exist, at least in the monkey and cat brain. They propose a genetic explanation for the development of such cells claiming that the mechanism responsible is genetic predetermination, i.e., cells in the visual cortex are prewired for orientation selectivity. Von der Malsburg (1973) proposes an alternative neural net solution to the development of orientation selectivity based on self-organizing neural nets. As he points out, one problem with a strong genetic predetermination hypothesis is the experimental demonstrations showing that orientation selectivity can be modified by early learning experience (Blakemore and Cooper, 1970, Blakemore and Mitchell, 1973). Other workers such as Kohonen (1982, 1984) accept that genetic predetermination provides a self-organizing structure which may then be modified by sensory learning experience.

Program 2 includes procedures based on research by both von der Malsburg and Kohonen. The program is not a truly "biological" simulation because it is hardly likely that any animal will be presented with a convenient set of rotating bars in a fixed frame of reference. The point of the simulation is to provide a demonstration of one way in which orientation sensitive units can arise automatically.

Architecture of the net

The net consists of two layers with an input of 8 x 8 units (= 64 units) and an inhibitory cluster of eight units. The layer-to-layer units are all excitatory and are modified using the Stent-Singer rule. Weights within the eight unit competitive cluster are fixed but the pattern of inhibition is different from the system used in the introductory program. In the present program each unit inhibits neighbouring units with the level of inhibition varying as the distance between units increases. This is called a "Mexican hat" pattern of inhibition (Figure 8.4 and Figure 8.5) and is quite common in competitive learning systems.

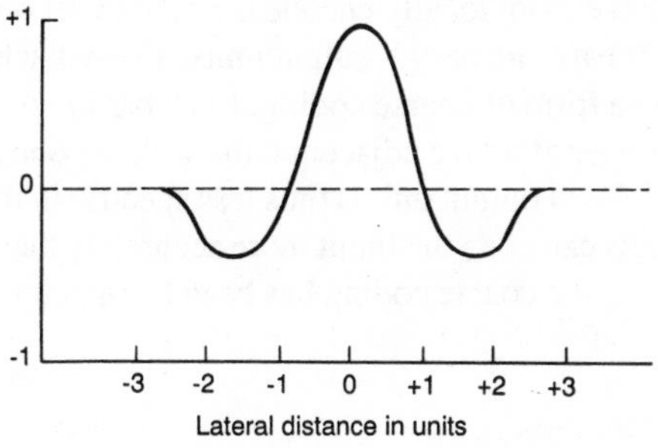

Figure 8.4. A typical Mexican hat operator which produces a differential pattern of inhibition based on lateral distance

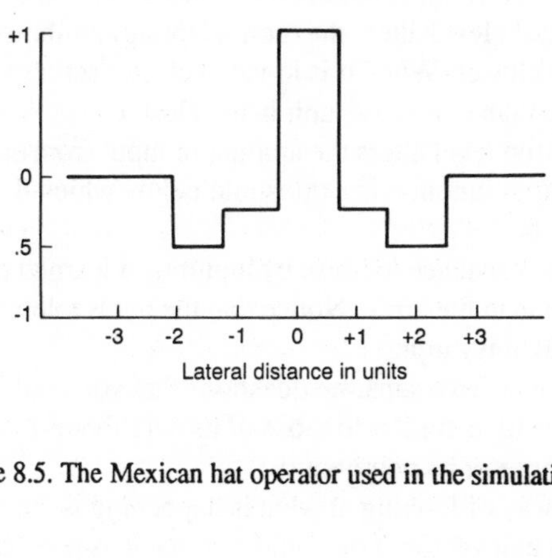

Figure 8.5. The Mexican hat operator used in the simulation

How to use the program

Select *Competitive Learning* from the main menu then select *Self-organising feature maps*. The program starts by displaying a template for the input with the initial random weights from all the input units to every output unit.

Select *Input* and click the mouse button nine times. The nine pattern inputs displayed correspond to a bar at different orientations.

Select *Learn*. The program will start cycling and will take a little time because so many weights (512) have to be updated on each cycle. After eight epochs some structure in the output should become apparent. As the number of epochs increases the structure of the weights becomes more obvious, shadowing the input.

The net learns to code the bars at different angles by a pattern of activity. No single unit codes a bar's precise angle: it is the collective activation which does this. Clearly, the net cannot locally encode the pattern set on a one-for-one basis because there are 9 bars and only 8 output units. The net achieves its organisation using a form of coarse coding. Each bar input produces an output consisting of a number of active adjacent units with the one in the middle most strongly activated. Each output unit is thus less specific in its meaning but the combination of units can code the input more accurately than a local representation. Once the coarse coding has been learned it is highly resistant to noisy input.

Exercises

Repeat exercises as in Program One. The net parameters can be adjusted, but note that as in Program 1 they can have a complex interdependence which makes the outcome of multiple parameter changes difficult to predict.

Inhibit: The inhibition level alters the (non-adapting) inhibition between the units in the competitive cluster. When it is low, the cluster settles very slowly and there may be more than one active unit in the cluster.

Excite: The excitation level alters the amount of input from each input unit.

Output fn: The output function is a threshold below which the unit does not output to other units.

Test: Test the net's resistance to noise by inputting a learned pattern with additional "on" units in the array. Notice that the net is tolerant of quite high levels of additional noisy input

Questions: There are two separate questions that you could think about. Why is a unit's receptive field similar to those of its neighbours? Why is its receptive field in between those of its neighbours?

Note that one way of looking at what is happening is the reduction from a 64 unit vector to an 8 unit vector. You could also see it as reducing the information in a 2-D array to a one-dimensional array.

Program Three: Build your own self-organising net

The program allows you to set up your own net and your own patterns. Each unit inhibits only its neighbour on each side (see Figure 8.2) by an amount specified with the inhibition parameter (*Inhib*). Each output unit (L2) can receive excitatory input from all cells to which it is connected in the input layer (L1) multiplied by the excitatory parameter (*Excit*). Layer-to-layer connections (L1 to L2) are all excitatory and can be adapted using either the Stent-Singer or the Rumelhart and Zipser learning rules.

The simulation is limited to ten output and ten input units. The nets are therefore very small compared with systems like the net for feature mapping but are useful for exploring basic principles. When deciding on net size you may note that it can be difficult to get competitive systems of this size and type to work with more than four or five units in the competitive cluster..

How to use the program

Select *Competitive Learning* from the main menu.
Select *Build your own Self-organising Net*, click *Continue*, then select the number of input and output units you want.
Select *Input* then specify the patterns. Filled input squares denote active units, blank squares are inactive. Should you make a mistake while you are specifying a pattern, don't forget that you can switch units either on or off by pointing at them. Input the pattern set you want the net to learn, then exit.

A pattern set to be learned can be input directly using the mouse, generated at random, or input from file. To generate new patterns at random simply click *Random*, and specify the proportion of units to be active, before clicking *Input*. Each click on *Input* will then bring in a new random pattern. To bring in a file of patterns to be learned click *Filer In* and then type the file name on the keyboard, in CAPITALS, ending with a carriage return. Each click on *Input* will then bring in the next pattern from the file. To save a pattern set for later use click *Filer Out*, and specify the file name on the keyboard, in CAPITALS, ending with a carriage return.

Select *Learn* and the program will start cycling. The amount of time it takes to learn any pattern set will depend on the size of the net, the number of patterns, and the relationships between patterns.

Exercises

Suggesting specific exercises for this program is difficult because the effectiveness of the system (i.e., how well it works) is very dependent on the number and ratio of input and output units, the input and the set of parameters. The parameters interact in a complex way and the outcome of any particular combination cannot easily be predicted in advance.

Several exercises and examples are given below and some guidelines are provided to help with your exploration of the net's characteristics.

Are contiguous receptive fields dependent on contiguous inputs?

Select a net with 8 input and 2 or 3 output units. Select *Input* and enter two different patterns in which alternating units are active. Select *Learn* and observe how the receptive fields develop. Note that in contrast to Exercise One in Program One, the receptive fields are not contiguous. Why is this so?

Critical periods for learning

Select a net with 9 input units and 3 output units. Select *Input* and then *Learn* the following patterns one at a time.

Pattern One: Input units 1 2 3, learn for 50 epochs, then stop learning.
Pattern Two: Input units 4 5 6, learn for another 50 epochs and stop learning.
Pattern Three: Input units 7 8 9 and learn.

You should notice that the net is unable to learn Pattern Three. If you study the weights matrix you will be able to see why this is so.

This effect may be seen as a simple analogy to the common observation in neurobiology that removal of sensory input during the period when the sensory cortex is developing post-natally leads to a permanent loss in the ability to respond to that input.

Inhibition and lateral distance

The net uses simple lateral inhibition and as a consequence of this neighbouring receptive fields will be different but non-neighbouring receptive fields may be the same. To see this, select a net with 10 input units and 10 output units. Select *Filer In* and specify the file COMP1. Set *Inhib* to about 0.15, select *Learn* and run for about 20 epochs. Notice that the receptive fields for each adjacent output unit are quite different, while those of some non-adjacent units are quite similar.

Clusters are relative

Select a 10 input and 2 output net. Select Input and input two partly overlapping patterns (e.g 1 2 3, 2 3 4). If there are only two patterns then the net can learn to discriminate but the parameter settings (*Inhibit* and *Output fn*) are critical. Experiment with the parameters to find reliable performance. Why can the net learn on some occasions and not others?

Whether the two output units will learn to discriminate at all depends on how many other patterns there are. If there are two other patterns (e.g.6 7 8, 7 8 9) then the net will learn to discriminate between the two clusters (1 2 3, 2 3 4 and 6 7 8, 7 8 9). What the net learns is to discriminate the largest difference between clusters.

The previous exercise demonstrated that with the given input patterns and two output units the net can discriminate. To what extent is this due to 'forcing' the outcome by restricting output to only two units?

If 10 output units are used for the same exercise then the net can still perform in the same way, however the outcome is different depending on which learning rule is applied. Experiment with the pattern set and the two learning rules. Why is the outcome different for the two rules?

Classifying patterns

Consider the following set of five input patterns:

Pattern	1:	1 0 1 0 1 0
	2:	0 1 0 1 0 1
	3:	1 0 1 0 0 1
	4:	1 0 0 1 1 0
	5:	0 1 1 0 1 0

There are several ways of classifying these patterns into two output units.

Solution One: Pattern 2 is orthogonal to pattern 1, i.e. they don't share any units in the same activation state, whereas patterns 3,4 and 5 all share at least two active units with pattern 1. One classification could be: One output unit active for input patterns 1,3,4 & 5. The other output unit active for input pattern 1.

Solution Two: Patterns 4 and 5 both have adjacent active units but the other patterns do not. A second classification could be: One output unit active for input patterns 4 and 5. The other output unit active for input patterns 1,2 and 3.

Solution Three: It may be possible for patterns with two neighbouring inactive units to be classified together, which would give: One output unit active for input patterns 3 and 4. The other output unit active for input patterns 1,2 and 5.

What happens in practice is that any of these solutions (and others) may occur. This is because the net organizes itself and the solution for any particular instance starts from a random weight setting. Thus even if the net parameters and input patterns are the same, different classifications will be produced over a number of trials.

Guidelines for further exercises

The following notes are intended to help you explore the net's characteristics and capabilities, with whatever patterns you choose. The pattern set should also be run a number of times using different parameter settings. To do this select *Options*, *Reset Weights*, then *Learn*.

Input patterns

The system should be able to classify any set of input patterns especially if you adjust the net parameters to help it along. Pattern sets which have only a few active units, say between 20% and 50% (also called a sparse input vector) tend to work better than pattern sets which have 80% to 90% active units. Pattern sets should also have some correlation or systematic relationship so that you have some idea of the output you would expect.

Inhibitory cluster

If none of the cluster units become active than no learning can take place (Remember that for both rules, weights are only changed on connections with active output units). To correct this decrease the *Output fn* parameter. This will decrease the "threshold" between cluster unit activation and output units. Additionally or alternatively the excitation parameter can be increased which will increase facilitation to cluster units and then to output units. If too many output units come on, then as well as decreasing the activation level (by decreasing the excitatory parameter) the inhibition parameter can be increased to raise the mutual inhibition within the inhibitory cluster and reducing the number of active output units.

Weight change parameters

These are best kept quite small. The best ratio of weight increment (*Wt Inc*) to weight decrement (*Wt Dec*) is very dependent on the type of input patterns you are using. Generally, if most of the input units are off (inactive) for every pattern in the set, then the weight increment should exceed the weight decrement. Conversely, if most input units are on then decrement should exceed increment. The balance situation is between the two extremes of overwhelming the inhibitory cluster with too much facilitation and starving it of facilitation.

Suggestions for further reading

The neural net simulations for this chapter are based partly on the article "Feature Discovery by Competitive Learning" by Rumelhart and Zipser (1986). Systems similar to the competitive learning described in this chapter have been developed by Rosenblatt (1962), von der Malsburg (1973), Fukushima (1975), Grossberg (1976) and Kohonen (1984).

9

Position Invariance

In a world of moving objects it is realistic and efficient to have separate representations of the position and identity of things. Functional specialisations arising from this distinction are common in nervous systems. In the mammalian neo-cortex posterior parietal regions deal with the positions of things and infero-temporal regions deal with their identity. However, in the retinal image, and in the various retinotopic maps, information about position and identity is combined. Cells are only activated by features of the right type *and* position on the retina. Thus a change in the position of an image on the retina can completely change the sets of cells that are activated in the various retinotopic maps. This is important because the effects of activity in a population of cells depends upon which cells are active. They will treat a new stimulus like an old one only to the extent that it activates the same cells as the old one. Thus if we want knowledge acquired about an object imaged at one position on the retina to transfer to images of that object at new positions then there must be a population of cells whose activity is determined by shape but not position. Input must be mapped into this population so that the same or similar shapes will activate the same or similar sets of cells wherever they appear on the retina. Saying that a shape stays the same means that the relations between its parts stays the same even though their relation to the retina changes. The problem therefore is to abstract the relations that are intrinsic to the shape from their extrinsic relations to the viewer with which they combine to form the image.

The system in this module is based on a program originally written by Geoffrey Hinton. An outline of the system and the motivation for it are given in Hinton (1981a). A valuable discussion of the theoretical issues involved is given in Hinton (1981b). The general approach is further developed and related to psychological phenomena in Hinton and Lang (1985) and Hinton and Parsons (1988).

In addition to knowing what things are and where things are it is necessary to know what things are where. That is if the representations of shape and position are separate they must also be linked appropriately. This is one example of what is generally known as the binding problem. The system presented in this module was not designed to show how this problem can be solved but it is compatible with a number of different possible solutions (Hinton, 1981b).

One way to abstract the relations that are intrinsic to the object is to use a frame of reference that is based upon the object itself rather than one that is based upon the retina. Relative to such a frame, the horizontal bar in a "T", for example, could then be described as being at the top, independently of where it is on the retina. Object-based frames of reference play an important role in many theories of visual perception. For example, in the theory of David Marr (1982) object recognition is achieved by mapping a viewer-centred representation onto a 3-D object centred representation.

The image of an object can also vary in size and orientation on the retina. The approach proposed by Hinton is intended to provide a shape representation that is also invariant over all of these changes, and orientation invariance is emphasized. However, his original simulation, Mapper, on which this module is based, provides only position invariance. It is its use in that role on which we concentrate here. This emphasis can be justified on the grounds that position invariance is the most basic. Contrary to what is usually assumed, psychological evidence shows that object recognition in humans and other animals is *not* in general independent of orientation (e.g., Rock, 1973).

If an object-based frame of reference is to be used to achieve generalisation across position, then there must be a way of selecting the appropriate frame. This will present a chicken-and-egg problem if we need to know what the object is in order to select the frame, because the role of the frame is to help decide what the object is. Hinton (1981a) says,

"The central problem in using object-based frames is to devise a way of assigning the appropriate frame to a perceived object. This is not an easy task, even if sources of information like stereo, shape-from shading, or optical flow have yielded the precise 3-D structure of the object relative to the frame of reference. Heuristics like planes of bilateral symmetry, gross elongation, and the gravitational or contextual vertical can help to suggest candidate object-based frames, but the final choice between the alternatives often depends on which object-based frame gives rise to a familiar shape description. An upside-down table, for example, is seen as just that, because by seeing it as upside-down we can see it as a familiar shape."

Hinton suggests that this problem can be solved by a parallel cooperative computation in a neural network, which settles on both the reference frame and the shape description at the same time. In this computation top-down and bottom-up influences cooperate to select the best mapping from input to object description.

Program One: Introduction to Mapper

This program provides a simulation of the cooperative neural computation just described. It enables patterns to be drawn onto a simple array of retinotopic units, and then shows how they are mapped onto an array of object-based units, and recognised as familiar shapes. When an input is presented all possible mappings into the object frame occur initially, and then compete with each other. The mappings that create familiar shape descriptions are strengthened and the others are weakened. Eventually the best mappings win. The strengths of the interactions within and between the various populations of units, and the rate at which their activations change can be varied, enabling you to study how these parameters affect the dynamics of the net.

How to use the program

The control panel is at the top of the screen provides the following functions.
Clear mappings resets activations to their default starting values.
Input presents or changes a stimulus.
Map starts or stops the relaxation cycles.
New shapes adds to the set of familiar shapes.
Parameters changes the parameter settings. (The default values to which they are automatically set produce useful behaviour in many cases).
Options allows you to exit or restart the module. It also allows you to specify the activity levels for individual mapping and shape units. Select either *Change Mappings* or *Help Shapes*, then specify a unit and type in its new activation level (a number followed by the return key). Use *Continue* to return to the main control panel.

Architecture of the network

There are four groups of units in Hinton's system:
1) a retinotopic frame with 10 x 10 units (A);
2) an object-based frame with 5 x 5 units (B);
3) an array of 10 x 10 mapping units (C);
4) one unit (E) for each familiar shape (D).

The small 5 x 5 arrays with filled circles show the four initial familiar shapes. The filled circles can also be viewed as excitatory connections between the corresponding object units and the "grandmother cells" at the top. Activity in the shape units is supported by and supports activity in the object units to which they are connected.

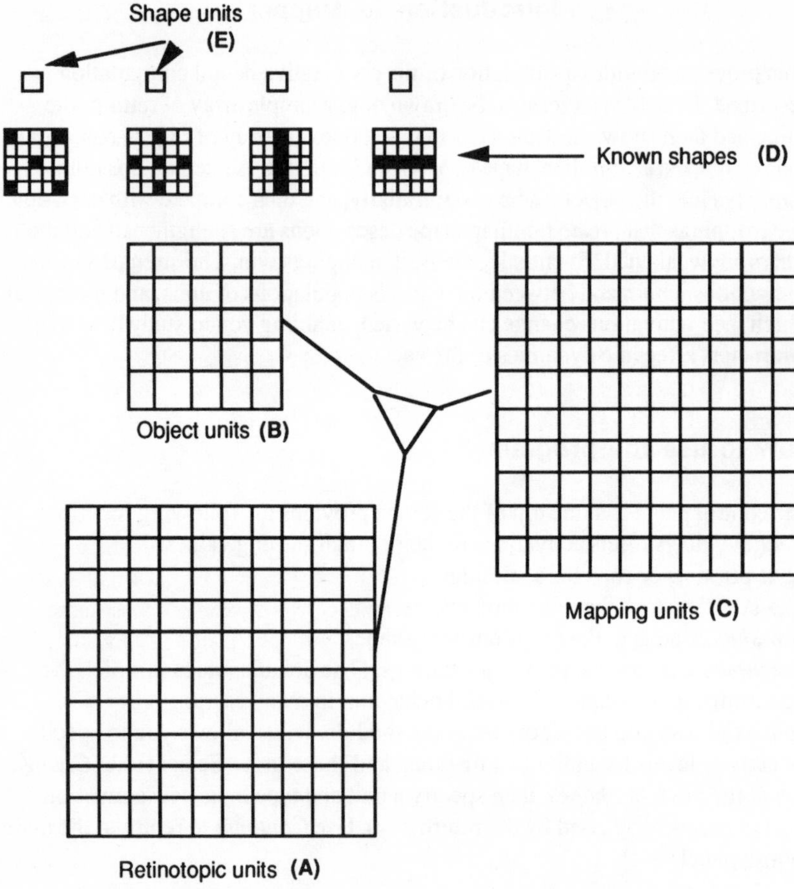

Figure 9.1. Hinton's mapping architecture for position invariance

Only one feature type is represented in this simulation. Activity in the retinotopic units shows the positions relative to the retina in which the feature is present, and activity in the object units shows the positions relative to the object in which the feature is present. In real nervous systems the conversion to an object-based frame would not happen until a fairly late stage of processing, and will involve many different feature types, such as oriented contours, corners, and line endings, etc.

Each mapping unit is associated with one possible mapping between the object and retinal frames. For example, one possible mapping is where the unit in the top left-hand corner of the retinal frame maps into the unit in the top left-hand corner of the object frame, and all of the 24 other units in the 5 x 5 array map accordingly. These 25 links are all supported by the mapping unit that is 3 down from the top and three in from the left on the mapping plane. Thus each mapping unit shows where the centre of the 5 x 5 object array should be placed on the retinal plane. This means that for some of the mapping units there are less than 25 links. The very top left-hand unit of the mapping plane for example only links the bottom right-hand 3 x 3 segment of the object plane to the retinal plane. Altogether the 100 mapping units provide 1,936 links between retinal and object units. The triangle linking these three groups of units stands for the way in which they support each other. This can be described by two rules:

1. Multiply the activity level in the retinotopic unit by the activity level in the mapping unit and send the product to the object unit specified by that mapping.
2. Multiply the activity level in the retinal unit by the activity in the object unit and send the product to the mapping unit that links them.

The first rule ensures a single coherent mapping when a single mapping unit is fully active. The second specifies which mapping unit should be active when the activity of the object units is determined from the top-down. These rules therefore use an activation function that differs from that used in all the previous modules.

Retinal activation is fixed as specified by the input. Activation of the other units evolves through deterministic synchronous cycles of interaction between the units. Each cycle has four main components: calculation of the excitatory input from the other groups; summing of this with a specified proportion of the units previous activation; setting to zero all activations less than a specified threshold; and normalising activations within the shape and mapping units so that within each group their sum equals 1.

The detailed dynamics of the net is controlled by three sets of parameters, all of which can be given values between 1 and 0: links, inertias, and thresholds:

Links

Four parameters control the strengths of the interactions between the different groups of units: from mapping and retinal units to object units; from object and retinal units to mapping units; from object to shape units; and from shape to object units.

Inertias

Three parameters, one for each group of units, determine the inertia of the units, i.e. how rapidly their activations change: the higher it is the slower they change. They specify the proportion of previous activation to be added to current input.

Thresholds

Three parameters, one for each group of units, set the thresholds. These determine the competition within groups. If the threshold is set so that only one unit is above it then the group becomes a winner-take-all net. The best value for this threshold varies. In general it should start low, e.g. 0.03, and increase slowly, e.g. to 0.2, as the relaxation cycles proceed. If no unit exceeds the threshold then it is not applied. Thus setting the threshold too high is equivalent to not having one at all.

Exercises

Mapping an unfamiliar shape into the object frame

Input any one of the familiar shapes, and then begin the mapping. In about 10 cycles the net will stabilise. The relaxation cycles can be stopped using the mouse button. The input pattern will then be shown correctly aligned in the object frame. The most active mapping unit will show where in the input array would make the best centre of the 5 x 5 to be mapped. Other active mapping units show other centres that link some of the active retinal and object units. Because of these subsidiary mappings the cross pattern in this example will show some weak redundant activity in the object frame. The next exercise shows how this can be overcome.

Sharpening mapping activity

Repeat Exercise 1 but after 10 cycles select *Parameters* and increase the mapping threshold parameter to 0.1, and then after a few more cycles increase it again to 0.15. This parameter sets the threshold below which a mapping unit's activity is switched off altogether. Thus gradually increasing this threshold will eliminate the weaker mapping units and eventually leave just a single active mapping. This single unit can be seen as a local code for the position of the centre, whereas the unsharpened activity can be seen as a distributed code. In many of the following exercises mapping can be sharpened by gradually increasing the mapping threshold. The greater the number of mapping units initially selected, the more gradual should be the increase. This is because the summed activity of all the mapping units is always set to 1. Therefore the more there are active the less activation there will be for each unit (remember also that the threshold is not applied at all if it is set so high that nothing exceeds it).

Disambiguating an input pattern by top-down information

Select *New Shapes* to specify a new shape consisting of a vertical column of five dots in the left-hand column of the 5 x 5 array. Input a vertical column of five dots on the retina. This input is completely ambiguous as to which familiar pattern it should be seen as. However, from the default start state this will be interpreted as a central column, because that has most units in common with other familiar patterns. Now repeat the above except that immediately prior to starting the mapping cycles set the activation of the new left-hand column shape unit to 0.5 using *Options* and *Help Shapes*. This "top-down" priming information is sufficient to change the interpretation to the non-dominant one.

Processing moving patterns

Select *Restart* to start the module, select *Input* and input a column of dots, then select *Map* and run 10 mapping cycles. Then using *Input* again, and without clearing the mappings or making any other changes, move the column one unit along its length. The net will now adjust to the new input and stabilise within only 2 mapping cycles. The adjustment only involves changes in the mapping units. This adjustment is less smooth if the mapping thresholds on the initial processing of the line are gradually increased to produce local codes for the position of the centre of the pattern to be mapped. This is because with a distributed representation of the position of the figure in the mapping plane, the activity required to represent its new position is already partly used to represent the old position.

Program Two:
Hinton's Mapper II

This program is identical to the introductory program except that it does not start with a default set of familiar shapes already specified. You must therefore ensure that at least one familiar shape is specified. You do this by using the instruction *Shapes*. The familiar shapes can include a blank matrix.
Select *Mapper II* from the *Position Invariance* menu.

Exercises

Mapping a single active input unit

Select *Shapes* and specify a single familiar shape consisting of a diagonal arrow pointing into one of the corners. Input (select *Input*) a single dot and start the mapping (select *Map*). The resulting activity in the object and mapping units is a good demonstration of the effects of the links in this system. The object unit activity simply reflects the familiar pattern. The mapping unit activity shows all possible centres of object frame relative to the retinal frame that link the single active retinal unit to an active object unit. Next see what happens when the effect of the familiar shape is removed by setting the "object to shape" parameter to 0. The single dot is still not mapped appropriately into the object frame. It is possible to achieve a good mapping by an appropriate setting of the "shape to object" parameter and use of the *Change Mappings* instruction. Can you discover how to do this?

Learning new patterns

So far we have not discussed how this system could map unfamiliar shapes into the object frame so that they can be learned. The previous exercise gives an example of the problem to be solved. To study this further select *Shapes* to specify one simple familiar shape such as a single dot at the centre of the 5 x 5. Input a C shape on the retina. You will find that if the C fits exactly into a 5 x 5 frame then a good mapping can be achieved with only a gradual increase of the mapping threshold from a starting value of 0.03 to about 0.1. If the C is too big to fit into a 5 x 5 frame mapping cannot be achieved with this system. If the C is smaller than a 5 x 5 then mapping can be achieved if you use *Change Mappings* to tell the mapping plane where the centre of the pattern is. This suggests that this system would be usefully enhanced by bottom-up processing telling the mapping units the position of figures on the retina.

Processing more complex scenes

Input (select *Input*) a familiar shape and add a number of dots haphazardly over the rest of the retina. With more dots in the input the mapping threshold should start lower, at about 0.015. You will find that the net often makes a good job of finding the familiar pattern in the noise. However, one weakness is that it also tries to find a 5 x 5 region of the retina with as many dots as possible, and this can override familiarity.

You could also try scenes with more than one familiar pattern. One way of doing this is to return to the *Introduction to Hinton's Mapper.* Think of the retina as made-up of four 5 x 5 arrays, instead of the 10 x 10 array. Select *Input* and place a horizontal line in one of these 5 x 5 arrays and a vertical line in another. In this case Mapper will find two centres and combine the two lines in the object frame. This presents an example of the binding problem. There is nothing in the activity of the object, shape, or mapping units to show which centre goes with which line.

If two patterns are drawn on the retina and something gives one an advantage then only that pattern will be mapped into the object frame. This will very often be the case since many things can give one shape an advantage over another, e.g. having more dots, sharing more dots in common with other familiar shapes, having more axes of symmetry, being primed, and being in a primed location. All of these can be investigated using this module.

This system can therefore represent only one shape at a time, or two familiar shapes superimposed, but it cannot represent scenes consisting of distinct familiar shapes in specified spatial relations to each other. Hinton (1981b) and Hinton and Parsons (1988) discuss the possibility of overcoming this limitation by adding a higher level of Scene-based units.

Discussion of Hinton's Mapper

This system is presented as a plausible theory of the way in which humans abstract shape information (Hinton and Lang, 1985; Hinton and Parsons, 1988). Assessment of its psychological and physiological plausibility raises a number of important issues, many of which are unresolved. Here we briefly list some of the more important ones.

The way in which the familiar shapes are represented is not the point of the system. "Grandmother" cells are simply used for programming convenience. Any other way of enhancing familiar patterns of activity in the object units would do. As it stands the system can be seen as using both local and distributed codes for familiar patterns - local in the shape units and distributed in the object units. Read-out could be from either or both of these.

The mapping units become more useful and physiologically plausible if they are seen as having two roles: 1. Mapping groups of active retinal units into an object frame; and 2. Representing the position of groups of active retinal units. The question this raises is "what groups?" The following point suggests that it is not adequate to answer this by saying "Those groups that produce a familiar shape representation."

The system assumes that a set of familiar shapes are known, but does not say how they become known. In order to be able to learn new shapes there must be some way of mapping unfamiliar patterns of activity. Exercise 6 shows that the system does not perform well in this role. It also suggests that this limitation might be overcome by adding a component that tells the mapping units the position of the groups of active retinal units to be mapped. This would have to include unfamiliar groups. Bottom-up grouping processes could contribute to this, but how they should be incorporated into this system is not yet clear. One other issue that might be relevant to this problem is that of how analyses at different scales of spatial resolution should be related.

This system uses just a single feature type, which is either present or absent. This increases the number of false partial matches that the mapping units can find, and is neither psychologically nor physiologically plausible. The version developed by Hinton and Lang (1985) has a richer feature set but consequently involves many more units and links.

The number of links that any system of this sort needs is called the N^2 problem by Hinton (1981b). If each of N retinal units can be mapped into any one of N object units then N^2 links are required. He suggests various ways in which this might be overcome. The problem may not be as bad as he supposes, however, because there is psychological evidence that the complexity of conceptual or object representations are very much less then those of sensory representations (Phillips, 1974).

You will have noticed during the exercises that good performance often requires dynamic control of some of the parameters. How this would be provided in an autonomous system is unspecified.

A more fundamental problem with this system is that it uses a fixed 5 x 5 object array. Thus the object frame itself is fixed and what is dynamic is only its relation to the input. A more powerful system would also be able to select an appropriate object frame, but how this could be done is also unspecified.

Finally, there is the problem of the relations between the parts. The system is based upon object units that code the relation between the parts and the whole object. It makes no use of the relations between the parts themselves. The system will therefore not generalise well to cases where the relations between some of the parts is constant but their relation to the whole changes.

References

Primary source references

The three following references are primary source references for the Guide. They are referenced in the text as PDP Vols 1 or 2, and as Anderson and Rosenfeld (1988).

Rumelhart, D.E., McClelland, J.R., & the PDP Research Group. (1986). *Parallel distributed processing: Explorations in the microstructure of cognition. Volume 1: Foundations.* Cambridge, MA: MIT Press.

McClelland, J.R., Rumelhart, D.E., & the PDP Research Group. (1986). *Parallel distributed processing: Explorations in the microstructure of cognition. Volume 2: Psychological and biological models.* Cambridge, MA: MIT Press.

Anderson, J.A. & Rosenfeld, E. (1988). *Neurocomputing: Foundations of research.* Cambridge, MA. MIT Press.

Other references

Amit, D.J. (1989). *Modelling brain function.* Cambridge: Cambridge University Press.

Anderson, J.A. (1983). Cognitive and psychological computation with neural models. *IEEE Transactions on Systems, Man and Cybernetics*, SMC-13, 799-815.

Blakemore, C. & Cooper, G.F. (1970). Development of the brain depends on the visual enviroment. *Nature (London)*, *228*, 477-478.

Blakemore, C. & Mitchell, D.E. (1973). Enviromental modification of the visual cortex and the neural basis of learning and memory. *Nature (London)*, *241*, 467-468.

Churchland, P.S. (1986). *Neurophilosophy.* Cambridge, MA: MIT Press.

Cornsweet, T.N. (1970). *Visual perception.* New York: Academic Press.

Fukushima, K. (1975). Cognition: A self-organizing multilayered neural network. *Biological Cybernetics, 20,* 121-136.

Grossberg, S. (1976). Adaptive pattern classification and universal recoding: Part I. Parallel development and coding of neural feature detectors. *Biological Cybernetics, 23,* 121-134. See also Anderson & Rosenfeld (1988), Chapter 19, pp. 245-258.

Hebb, D.O. (1949). *The organisation of behaviour.* New York: Wiley. See also Anderson & Rosenfeld (1988), Chapter 4, pp. 45-56.

Hinton, G.E. (1981a). Implementing semantic networks in parallel hardware. In G.E. Hinton & J.A. Anderson (Eds.), *Parallel models of associative memory*. Hillsdale, NJ: Lawrence Erlbaum Associates.

Hinton, G.E. (1981b). A parallel computation that assigns canonical object-based frames of reference. *Proceedings of the 7th International Joint Conference on Artificial Intelligence.*

Hinton, G.E. & Anderson, J.A. (Eds.) (1981). *Parallel models of associative memory*. Hillsdale, NJ: Lawrence Erlbaum Associates.

Hinton, G.E. & Lang, K. (1985). Shape recognition and illusory conjunctions. *Proceedings of the 9th International Joint Conference on Artificial Intelligence*, 252-260.

Hinton, G.E. & Parsons, L.M. (1988). Scene-based and viewer centred representations for comparing shapes. *Cognition, 30*, 1-35.

Hinton, G.E. & Sejnowski, T.J. (1986). Learning and relearning in Boltzmann machines. In: *PDP Vol. 1*, pp. 282-317.

Hopfield, J.J. (1982). Neural networks and physical systems with emergent collective computational abilities. *Proceedings of the National Academy of Sciences, 79*, 2554-2558. See also Anderson & Rosenfeld (1988), Chapter 27, pp. 460- 464.

Hopfield, J.J. (1984). Neurons with graded response have collective computational properties like those of two-state neurons. *Proceedings of the National Academy of Sciences, 81*, 3088-3092. See also Anderson & Rosenfeld (1988), Chapter 35, pp. 579-584.

Hubel, D.H. & Weisel, T.N. (1962). Receptive fields, binocular interaction and functional architecture in the cat's visual cortex. *Journal of Physiology, 160*, 106-154.

Hubel, D.H. & Weisel, T.N. (1963). Receptive fields of cells in straite cortex of very young, visually inexperienced kittens. *Journal of Neurophysiology, 26*, 994-1002.

Knapp, A.G. & Anderson, J.A. (1984). Theory of categorisation based on distributed memory storage. *Journal of Experimental Psychology, 10*, 616-637.

Knight, K. (1989). A gentle introduction to subsymbolic computation: Connectionism for the A.I. researcher. *Carnegie Mellon University School of Computer Science Technical Report CMU-CS-89-150.*

Kohonen, T. (1982). Self-organised formation of topologically correct feature maps. *Biological Cybernetics, 43*, 59-69. See also Anderson & Rosenfeld (1988), Chapter 30, pp. 511-522.

Kohonen, T. (1984). *Self-organisation and associative memory.* Heidelberg: Springer-Verlag.

Kohonen, T. (1987). *Self-organisation and associative memory.* Berlin: Springer-Verlag.

Lindsay, P.H. & Norman, D.A. (1972). *Human information processing.* New York: Academic Press.

Luria, A.R. (1973). *The working brain.* London: Penguin.

Marr, D. (1982). *Vision.* San Francisco: Freeman. See also Anderson & Rosenfeld (1988), Chapter 28, pp. 468-480.

McClelland, J.R. & Rumelhart, D.E. (1985). Distributed memory and the representation of general and specific information. *Journal of Experimental Psychology: General, 114*, 159-188. See also *PDP Vol. 2*, Chapter 17, pp. 170-215.

McClelland, J.R. & Rumelhart, D.E. (1986). A distributed model of human learning and memory. In *PDP Vol. 2*, Chapter 17, pp. 170-215.

McClelland, J.R. & Rumelhart, D.E. (1988). *Explorations in parallel distributed processing: A handbook of models, programs, and exercises.* Cambridge, MA: MIT Press.

McLaren, I.P.L., Kaye, H., & Mackintosh, N.J. (1989). An associative theory of the representation of stimuli: Applications to perceptual learning and latent inhibition. In R.G.M. Morris (Ed.), *Parallel Distributed Processing.* Oxford: Claredon Press.

Minsky, M. & Papert, S. (1969). *Perceptrons.* Cambridge, MA: MIT Press. See also Anderson & Rosenfeld (1988), Chapter 13, pp. 161-170.

Mountcastle, V.B. (1978). In E.M. Edelman & V.B. Mountcastle (Eds.), *The Mindful Brain*, pp. 7-50. Cambridge, MA: MIT Press.

Nadal, J. & Toulouse, G. (1990). Information storage in sparsely coded memory nets. *Network: Computation in neural systems, 1*, 61-74.

Phillips, W.A. & Singer, W. (1974). Function and interaction of on and off transients in vision: I. Psychophysics. *Experimental Brain Research, 19*, 493-506.

Pinker, S. & Prince, A. (1988). On language and connectionism: Analysis of a parallel distributed processing model of language acquisition. *Cognition, 28*, 73-194.

Posner, M.I. & Keele, S.W. (1970). Retention of abstract ideas. *Journal of Experimental Psychology, 83*, 304-308.

Prince, A. & Pinker, S. (1988). Rules and connections in human language. *Trends in the Neurosciences, 11*, 195-202.

Ratliff, F. (1965). *Mach Bands: Quantitative studies of neural networks in the retina.* San Francisco, CA: Holden-Day.

Rock, I. (1973). *Orientation and form.* New York: Academic Press.

Rockel, A.J., Hiorns, R.W., & Powell, T.P.S. (1980). The basic uniformity in structure of the neo-cortex. *Brain, 133*, 221-244.

Rosenblatt, F. (1962). *Principles of neurodynamics*. New York: Spartan.

Rumelhart, D.E., Hinton, G.E., & Williams, R.J. (1986). Learning representations by back-propagating errors. *Nature (London), 323*, 533-536. See also Anderson & Rosenfeld (1988), Chapter 42, pp. 696-700.

Rumelhart, D.E. & McClelland, J.R. (1986a). PDP models and general issues in cognitive science. In: *PDP Vol. 1,* Chapter 4, pp. 110-146.

Rumelhart, D.E. & McClelland, J.R. (1986b). On learning the past tenses of English verbs. In: *PDP Vol. 2,* Chapter 18, pp. 216-271.

Rumelhart, D.E. & Zipser, D. (1986). Feature discovery by competitive learning. In *PDP Vol. 1,* Chapter 5, pp. 151-193.

Sejnowski, T.J., Koch, C. & Churchland, P.S. (1988). Computational neuroscience. *Science*, 241, 1299-1306.

Singer, W. (1987). Activity-dependant self-organisation of synaptic connections as a substrate of learning. In J.P. Changeux, & M. Konishi (Eds.) *The Neural and Molecular Bases of Learning*. London: Wiley.

Singer, W. & Phillips, W.A. (1974). Function and interaction of on and off transients in vision II. Neurophysiology. *Experimental Brain Research, 19*, 507-521.

Spillman, L. & Werner, J.S. (Eds.) (1990). *Visual perception: The neurophysiological foundations.* San Diego, CA: Academic Press Inc.

Stanton, P. & Sejnowski, T.J. (1989). Associative long-term depression in the hippocampus: Induction of synaptic plasticity by Hebbian covariance. *Nature (London), 339*, 215-218.

Stent,G.S. (1973). A physiological mechanism for Hebb's postulate of learning. *Proceedings of the National Academy of Sciences, 70*, 997-1001.

Sutton, R.S. & Barto, A.G. (1981). Toward a modern theory of adaptive networks: expectation and prediction. *Psychological Review, 88*, 135-170.

Tank, D.W. & Hopfield, J.J. (1987). Collective computation in neuronlike circuits. *Scientific American, 257*, 62-70.

von Bekesy, G. (1967). *Sensory inhibition.* Princeton, NJ: Princeton University Press.

von der Malsburg, C. (1973). Self-organizing of orientation sensitive cells in the straite cortex. *Kybernetik, 14*, 85-100. See also Anderson & Rosenfeld (1988), Chapter 17, pp. 212-228.

von Neumann, J. (1958). The computer and the brain. New Haven: Yale University Press, pp. 66-82. See also Anderson & Rosenfeld (1988), Chapter 7, pp 83-88.

Watt, R, J. (1988). *Visual Processing: Computational, psychological and cognitive research.* Hove: Lawrence Erlbaum Associates Ltd.

Willshaw, D. & Dayan, P. (1990). Optimal plasticity from matrix memories: What goes up must come down. *Neural Computation, 2*, 85-93.

Zipser, D. (1990). Modelling cortical computation with backpropagation. In M.A. Gluck & D.E. Rumelhart (Eds.), *Neuroscience and connectionist theory*, pp. 355-38). Hillsdale: Lawrence Erlbaum Associates.

Appendix 1: Auto-association

Hebbian rules

The module uses rules based on a formulation for learning devised by Donald Hebb in 1949. Basic Hebbian rules are the simplest form of learning rules introduced in this guide. Learning takes place by modifying weights on connections between units; the activation states of the pre-synaptic and post-synaptic units determine the modification of the weights.

For the sake of simplicity and ease of comprehension we illustrate the rule for just one pattern (p) which removes the need for an extra subscript in the equations below. Let us assign the subscript j to denote operations within each unit of the net and the subscript i to denote the output from each unit to all the other units in the net. Post-synaptic activation therefore has a j subscript and pre-synaptic activation has an i subscript.

The Hebbian auto-associators have two main modes of processing. One of these is Learning (often called Training) during which the weights on connections between units are adjusted. The other mode is Testing where a pattern is presented to the net and the output from the net is computed. Weights are not adapted during testing.

The auto-associative programs use six different rules for learning and these are treated in two sections for Program One, and for Programs Two and Three.

Learning

During learning a set of patterns is presented to the net one at a time. The weights on connections between the units in the net are modified for each pattern separately. The weight changes are cumulative.

Program 1

This program uses the simplest form of Hebbian learning with the following three rules:

Hebb rule: Weights on connections are changed only when the post-synaptic unit (a_j)is active. If the pre-synaptic unit (o_i)is active then the weight on the connection between them is increased by an increment of 1.

$$w_{ij} = w_{ij}+1 \text{ if } a_j = 1 \text{ and } o_i = 1$$

Stent-Singer rule: Weights on connections are changed only when the post-synaptic unit is active. If the pre-synaptic unit is active then the weight on the connection between them is increased by an increment of 1. If the pre-synaptic unit is inactive then the weight on the connection between them is decreased by a decrement of 1.

$$w_{ij} = w_{ij}+1 \text{ if } a_j = 1 \text{ and } o_i = 1$$
$$w_{ij} = w_{ij}-1 \text{ if } a_j = 1 \text{ and } o_i = 0$$

Hopfield rule: If the post-synaptic unit is in the same state of activation as the pre-synaptic unit then the connection weight between them is increased by an increment of 1. If the post-synaptic unit is in a different state of activation to the pre-synaptic unit then the connection weight between them is decreased by a decrement of 1.

$$w_{ij} = w_{ij}+1 \text{ if } a_j = 1 \text{ and } o_i = 1$$
$$w_{ij} = w_{ij}+1 \text{ if } a_j = 0 \text{ and } o_i = 0$$
$$w_{ij} = w_{ij}-1 \text{ if } a_j = 0 \text{ and } o_i = 1$$
$$w_{ij} = w_{ij}-1 \text{ if } a_j = 1 \text{ and } o_i = 0$$

Programs 2 and 3

The three learning rules used in these programs are the post-synaptic rule, the pre-synaptic rule and the Covariance rule.

The post-synaptic rule: Weights on connections are changed only when the post-synaptic unit (a_j) is active. If the pre-synaptic unit (o_i) is active then the weight on the connection between them is increased by the *Wt Inc++* parameter (A). If the pre-synaptic unit is inactive then the weight on the connection between them is decreased by the *Wt Dec* parameter (C).

$$w_{ij} = w_{ij}+A \text{ if } a_j = 1 \text{ and } o_i = 1$$
$$w_{ij} = w_{ij}-C \text{ if } a_j = 1 \text{ and } o_i = 0$$

The pre-synaptic rule: Weights on connections are changed only when the pre-synaptic unit (o_i) is active. If the post-synaptic unit (a_j) is active then the weight on the connection between them is increased by the *Wt Inc++*

parameter (A). If the pre-synaptic unit is inactive then the weight on the connection between them is decreased by the *Wt Dec* parameter (C).

$$w_{ij} = w_{ij}+A \text{ if } a_j= 1 \text{ and } o_i = 1$$
$$w_{ij} = w_{ij}-C \text{ if } a_j = 0 \text{ and } o_i = 1$$

The covariance rule: As its name implies, the weight change depends on the relative activity state of the the pre-synaptic and post-synaptic units. If both the post-synaptic and pre-synaptic units are active then the weight is increased by the *Wt Inc++* parameter (A). If they are both inactive then the *Wt Inc00* parameter (B) is used. If the two units are in different states of activation then the weight is decremented by the *Wt Dec* parameter (C).

$$w_{ij} = w_{ij}+A \text{ if } a_j = 1 \text{ and } o_i = 1$$
$$w_{ij} = w_V+B \text{ if } a_j = 0 \text{ and } o_i = 0$$
$$w_{ij} = w_{ij} -C \text{ if } a_j = 0 \text{ and } o_i = 1$$
$$w_{ij} = w_{ij} -C \text{ if } a_j = 1 \text{ and } o_i = 0$$

Testing the net

During the test mode a test pattern is presented to the net and the activation of each unit is computed (a cycle). The output of each unit is then fed back to the other units in the net and the activation of each unit is then recalculated. This procedure continues over a number of cycles.

To calculate the activation of each unit

First, let us determine the net input to unit j (net_j). We can distinguish between external (e_j) and internal input (I_j). External input comes from outside the net, internal input is input from other units within the net.

The internal input to a unit is equal to the output (o_i) of each of the other units multiplied by the weight at the connections with those units;

$$I_j = \Sigma_i(o_i w_{ij})$$

I_j stands for the internal input to unit j. The subscript i stands for the ith unit in the net. The summation indicated by Σ is over all n units in the net. W_{ij} is the weight on the connection from unit i to unit j.

The net input (net_j) to each unit is equal to the external input plus the total internal input;

$$net_j = I_j+e_j$$

The activation states range between values of 0 and 1 and are bounded. The activation of a unit is equal to the net input as long as this condition is satisfied. The output (o_j) of each unit is equal to the activation.

$$a_j = net_j \text{ if } 0 > net_j > 1$$
$$a_j = 0 \text{ if } net_j < 0$$
$$a_j = 1 \text{ if } net_j > 1$$
$$o_j = a_j$$

The Delta rule

The notes in this appendix should be supplemented by reference to the original paper (McClelland and Rumelhart, 1985) where the model is fully specified. The desired state for an auto-associative memory is for it to be able to store and retrieve a number of different patterns from within the same weights matrix, if this is possible. There are two modes of processing under the Delta rule; a Learning mode and a Test mode.

Learning: The delta rule operates by determining the difference (or error) between the actual output for each pattern and the desired output for each pattern. This is achieved by using a number of processing cycles, where on each cycle during learning small adjustments are made to the weights to minimise the error between actual and desired output. The processing cycles continue until the error for each pattern is acceptably close to zero.

Each learning cycle has four stages: 1) each unit determines its net input: 2) the activation of the unit is updated: 3) the difference, or error, between actual and desired output is computed: and 4) if there is an error the weights at connections with other units are modified to reduce the error by a small amount.

Testing the net: Testing involves processing of a test pattern through stages 1) to 3) of the learning procedure. Weights are not updated during test. For the sake of simplicity and ease of comprehension we illustrate the rule for just one pattern (p) which removes the need for an extra subscript in the equations below.

Learning

Step 1: Determine net input to each unit

First, let us determine the net input (net_j) to each unit. We can distinguish between external (e_j) and internal input (i_j). External input comes from outside the net (i.e. it is the pattern the net is trying to learn), internal input is input from other units within the net.

The internal input to a unit is equal to the output (o_j) of each of the other units multiplied by the weight at the connections with those units;

$$I_j = \Sigma_i(o_j w_{ij})$$

The net input (net_j) to each unit is equal to the external input plus the total internal input;

$$net_j = I_j + e_j$$

Step 2: Compute and update the activation for each unit

Calculate the change in the activation level. This is accomplished by multiplying the net input by an excitation parameter (E) and by a function of the old activation of the unit minus a decay parameter (D);

$$\Delta a_j = E net_j(1-a_j)-Da_j \quad \text{if } net_j>0$$
$$\Delta a_j = E net_j(a_j+1)-Da_j \quad \text{if } net_j<0$$

The new activation is the sum of the old activation plus the change in the activation.

$$a_j = \Delta a_j + a_j$$

Step 3: Cycle the activation (relaxation)

Repeat steps 2 and 3 for M cycles where M=50 for learning and M=30 for test.

Step 4: Calculate the error

Calculate the difference (δ) between the external input and the internal input. In the case of an auto-associative net in its learning phase, the external input to the net is the same as the desired output of the net.

$$\delta_j = e_j - I_j$$

Step 5: Update the weights

If there is an error then the change in the weights at connections with each of the other units is equal to a proportion (specified by the learning rate, S) of the error multiplied by the activation of those units;

$$w_{ij} = S\delta_j a_j$$

Appendix 2: Pattern Association

Hebbian rules

The programs use Hebbian learning rules similar to those in Appendix 1. Learning takes place by modifying weights on connections between units; the activation states of the pre-synaptic and post-synaptic units determine the modification of the weights.

The Hebbian pattern associators also have two main modes of processing, similar to the Hebbian auto-associators (see Appendix 1): Learning during which the weights on connections between units are adjusted and Testing where a pattern is presented to the net and the output from the net is computed. Weights are not adapted during testing.

Let us assign the subscript i to units in L1 and the subscript j to units in L2. For the sake of simplicity and ease of comprehension we illustrate the rule for just one pattern (p) which removes the need for an extra subscript in the equations below. Post-synaptic activation therefore has a j subscript and pre-synaptic activation has an i subscript.The rules operate as follows:

Learning

During learning a set of patterns is presented to the net one at a time. The weights on connections between the input units (L1) and the output units which receive the training signal (L2) are modified for each pattern separately. The weight changes are cumulative.

To determine the weights: The Hebbian pattern associators use six different rules altogether and these are treated in two sections for Program 1, and for Program 2.

Program 1

This program uses the simplest form of Hebbian learning with the following three rules:

Hebb rule: Weights on connections are changed only when the post-synaptic unit (a_j) in L2 is active. If the pre-synaptic unit in L1 is active then the weight on the connection between them is increased by an increment of 1.(o_i = the output from the input unit.)

$$w_{ij} = w_{ij}+1 \quad \text{if } a_j = 1 \text{ and } o_i = 1$$

Stent-Singer rule: Weights on connections are changed only when the post-synaptic unit (a_j in L2) is active. If the pre-synaptic unit (o_i in L1) is also active then the weight on the connection between them is increased by an increment of 1. If the pre-synaptic unit is inactive then the weight on the connection between them is decreased by an decrement of 1.

$$w_{ij} = w_{ij}+1 \quad \text{if } a_j = 1 \text{ and } o_i = 1$$
$$w_{ij} = w_{ij}-1 \quad \text{if } a_j = 1 \text{ and } o_i = 0$$

Hopfield rule: If the post-synaptic unit (a_j) is in the same state of activation as the pre-synaptic unit (o_i) then the connection weight between them is increased by an increment of 1. If the post-synaptic unit is in a different state of activation to the pre-synaptic unit then the connection weight between them is decreased by a decrement of 1.

$$w_{ij} = w_{ij}+1 \quad \text{if } a_j = 1 \text{ and } o_i = 1$$
$$w_{ij} = w_{ij}+1 \quad \text{if } a_j = 0 \text{ and } o_i = 0$$
$$w_{ij} = w_{ij}-1 \quad \text{if } a_j = 0 \text{ and } o_i = 1$$
$$w_{ij} = w_{ij}-1 \quad \text{if } a_j = 1 \text{ and } o_i = 0$$

Program Two: Build your own net

The three learning rules used in these programs are the post-synaptic rule, the pre-synaptic rule and the Covariance rule.Hebbian rules in this section may be seen as more developed versions of the previous rules.

The post-synaptic rule: Weights on connections are changed only when the post-synaptic unit (a_j) is active. If the pre-synaptic unit (o_i) is active then the weight on the connection between them is increased by the *Wt 'Inc++* parameter (A). If the pre-synaptic unit is inactive then the weight on the connection between them is decreased by the *Wt Dec* parameter (C).

$$w_{ij} = w_{ij}+A \quad \text{if } a_j = 1 \text{ and } o_i = 1$$
$$w_{ij} = w_{ij}-C \quad \text{if } a_j = 1 \text{ and } o_i = 0$$

The pre-synaptic rule: Weights on connections are changed only when the pre-synaptic unit (o_i) is active. If the post-synaptic unit (a_j) is active then the weight on the connection between them is increased by the *Wt Inc++* parameter (A). If the pre-synaptic unit is inactive then the weight on the connection between them is decreased by the *Wt Dec* parameter (C).

$$w_{ij} = w_{ij}+A \quad \text{if } o_i = 1 \text{ and } a_j = 1$$
$$w_{ij} = w_{ij}-C \quad \text{if } o_i = 0 \text{ and } a_j = 1$$

The covariance rule: As its name implies, the weight change depends on the relative activity state of the the pre-synaptic and post-synaptic units.
If both the post-synaptic and pre-synaptic units are active then the weight is increased by the *Wt Inc++* parameter (A). If they are both inactive then the *Wt Inc00* parameter (B) is used. If the two units are in different states of activation then the weight is decremented by the *Wt Dec* parameter (C).

$$w_{ij} = w_{ij}+A \quad \text{if } a_j = 1 \text{ and } o_i = 1$$
$$w_{ij} = w_{ij}+B \quad \text{if } a_j = 0 \text{ and } o_i = 0$$
$$w_{ij} = w_{ij}-C \quad \text{if } a_j = 0 \text{ and } o_i = 1$$
$$w_{ij} = w_{ij}-C \quad \text{if } a_j = 1 \text{ and } o_i = 0$$

Testing the net

During the test mode a test pattern is presented to the net and the activation of each unit is computed (a cycle). The output of each unit is then fed back to the other units in the net and the activation of each unit is then recalculated. This procedure continues over a number of cycles.

To calculate the activation of each output unit in L2

The net input (net_j) is equal to the sum of the output from each input unit in L1 multiplied by the weight on its connection with the unit in L2 (o_i = the output from the input unit.).

$$net_j = \Sigma_i(o_i w_{ij})$$

The subscript i stands for the ith unit in the input. The summation indicated by Σ is over all n units in the net. W_{ij} stands for the weights on the connection from unit i in L1 to unit j in L2.

The activation states range between values of 0 and 1 and are bounded. The activation of a unit is equal to the net input as long as this condition is satisfied. The output (o_j) of each unit in L2 is equal to the activation.

$$a_j = net_j \text{ if } 0 > net_j > 1$$
$$a_j = 0 \text{ if } net_j < 0$$
$$a_j = 1 \text{ if } net_j > 1$$
$$o_j = a_j$$

The Delta rule

The program is derived from the paper "On Learning the Past Tenses of English Verbs" by Rumelhart and McClelland (1986b). We keep as closely as possible to their terminology for those users who wish to consult the paper while using our program simulations. There are two modes of processing under the Delta rule; a Learning mode and a Test mode.

Learning: Note that with the Delta rule the entire pattern set to be learned is presented to the net and weights are changed by a small amount for each pattern in turn and this procedure continues across a number of epochs. This aspect of the procedure is unlike the Hebbian procedures where weights are changed only once for each pattern in the pattern set. The Delta rule operates by determining the difference (or error) between the actual output for each pattern and the desired output for each pattern. This is achieved by using a number of processing cycles, where on each cycle during learning small adjustments are made to the weights to minimise the error between actual and desired output. The processing cycles continue until the error for each pattern is acceptably close to zero.

Testing the net: A pattern is presented to the net and the activation of units in the output layer (L2) is calculated by multiplying the inputs by the previously determined weights between the input (L1) and output (L2) layers.

For the sake of simplicity and ease of comprehension we illustrate the rule for just one pattern (p) which removes the need for an extra subscript in the equations below.

Two activation functions are possible and these are described below. The rule operates as follows:

Learning

Step 1: Calculate activation of each unit in L2

The net input (net_j) to each unit is equal to the sum of the values of each input (o_i) multiplied by the weight on its connection with L2 (o_i = the output from the input unit.)

$$net_j = \Sigma_i(w_{ij}o_i)$$

Linear activation function: The activation of each unit is equal to the net input but it is bounded at 0 and 1

$$a_j = net_j$$

Logistic activation function: The logistic activation function applied to the net input (net_j) is

$$a_j = \frac{1}{1+e^{-net_j}}$$

Step 2: Calculate the error

First calculate the difference (δ_j) between the actual output at L2 (a_j)and the target output (t_j)required

$$\delta_j = t_j - a_j$$

Step 3: Change the weights between L1 and L2

The weight change = learning rate (S) multiplied by the error (δ_j) multiplied by the activation (I_i) of the L1 input unit.

$$\Delta w_{ij} = S\, \delta_j I_i$$

Testing the net

To test the net, for each test pattern we calculate the activation and output of each unit in L2. This is the same as steps 1 and 2 in the Learning mode above.

Appendix 3: Backpropagation

For the sake of simplicity and ease of comprehension we illustrate the backpropagation rule for just one pattern (p) which removes the need for an extra subscript in the equations below. The description of the procedure is modelled on Rumelhart, Hinton and Williams' (1986) description and like them we equate activation and output for each unit. For a more detailed exposition see their article in PDP Volume 1 Chapter 8, pp 318-362.

Learning is achieved using two passes through the net. The first pass propagates the activation forward to compute a value for the output unit(s) in layer three (L3). In the second (backward) pass the error between the activation of the output unit(s) and the target output is calculated, the error is propagated back through the net and the error term is used to update the weights.

Testing the net involves one forward pass through the net to compute the activation and output at the output layer (L3).

In the following description we use the subscript i for units in layer one (L1), subscript j for units in layer two (L2), and subscript k for units in layer three (L3).

Learning: Forward pass to calculate unit activation levels in the hidden layer (L2) and the output layer (L3)

Step 1: Calculate the activation (a_j) for each unit in L2

First calculate the net input to each unit in L2. The net input = the sum of the unit activations in the input layer (a_i) multiplied by the weights on connections with L2, plus the bias on the L2 unit

$$net_j = \Sigma_i w_{ij} a_i + bias_j$$

The activation (a_j) of each unit in the hidden layer (L2) is equal to a logistic function applied to the net input

$$a_j = \frac{1}{1 + e^{-net_j}}$$

Step 2: Calculate the net input (net_k) for each unit in L3

The net input = the sum of the activations from L2 (a_k) multiplied by the weights on connections with L3, plus the bias on the L3 unit

$$net_k = \Sigma_j w_{jk} a_j + bias_k$$

Now calculate the activation (a_k) for each unit) in L3. The logistic activation function applied to the net input (net_k) is

$$a_k = \frac{1}{1 + e^{-net_k}}$$

Learning: Backward pass to compute the error term and update the weights

Step 1: Compute the derivative with respect to the net input of the error for each output unit in L3

δ_k is equal to the product of the target output (t_k) minus the activation (a_k), multiplied by the following function;

$$\delta_k = (t_k - a_k) a_k (1 - a_k)$$

Step 2: Change the weights between L2 and L3 (including the bias)

The weight change = learning rate (S) multiplied by the error (δ_i) multiplied by the activation (a_j) of the L2 unit.

$$\Delta w_{jk} = S\, \delta_k a_j$$

Note that when the momentum term (M) is included the weight change for the current presentation (n) of the pattern is added:

$$\Delta w_{jk}(n+1) = S(\delta_k a_j) + M\,\Delta w_{jk}(n)$$

Step 3: Calculate the error term for the hidden layer units in L2

First calculate the derivative of the activation for each hidden unit ($a_j(1-a_j)$), then multiply this by the sum of the error terms from the units in L3 (δ_k) and the sum of the weights between L2 and L3.

$$\delta_j = a_j(1-a_j)\Sigma_k\,\delta_k\,w_{jk}$$

Step 4: Change the weights between L1 and L2 (including the bias)

The weight change = learning rate (S) multiplied by the error from L2 (δ_j) multiplied by the activation (a_j) of the input unit. (which is either 0 or 1 in the present case).

$$\Delta w_{ij} = S\,\delta_j\,a_i$$

The whole procedure (forward and backward passes) is then repeated for the next pattern-pair in the sequence and continues until the error for each pattern is reduced to a level approaching zero. Given that the rule uses a logistic activation function, the error can never reach zero. A critical error level of 0.1 is commonly used as an acceptable value and learning is considered to have taken place once the error on all patterns is less than or equal to the critical error value.

Testing the net

A test pattern is presented to the net and the activation of the L3 output units is calculated using one forward pass through the net (Steps 1 and 2 in Forward Pass).

Appendix 4: Competitive Learning

For the sake of simplicity and ease of comprehension we illustrate the rule for just one pattern (p) which removes the need for an extra subscript in the equations below. Part of the procedure outlined is specified in more detail in the article "Feature Discovery by Competitive Learning" by Rumelhart and Zipser (PDP Volume 1, Chapter 5, pp 151-193).

The description which follows is of the learning procedure for Programs One and Three. The testing procedure is to compute the output at L2 ie. Steps 1 and 2 of the Learning procedure. Weights are not updated during testing.

Step 1: Compute the net input (net_j) to each unit in the competitive cluster (L2)

The net input to each unit in L2 is equal to the sum of the activation of each input unit (a_i) in L1 multiplied by the weight on its connection with L2.

$$net_j = \Sigma_i(w_{ij}a_i)$$

The subscript i stands for the ith unit in L1. The summation indicated by Σ is over all n input units in the net. W_{ij} stands for the weights on all connections from unit i in L1 to unit j in L2.

Step 2: Calculate the activation (a_j) and output (o_j) of each unit in L2

The activation of each unit is equal to its net input multiplied by the excitatory parameter (E) minus the output (o_j) of each adjacent unit multiplied by the inhibitory parameter (H).

$$a_j = (E\ net_j) - H(o_{j-1}) - H(o_{j+1})$$

The output of each unit is determined by the output function (F). If activation is greater than the output threshold (F) then the output (o_j) is equal to the activation. If activation is less than the output function then output is zero.

$$\text{If } a_j >= F \text{ then } (o_j) = a_j$$
$$\text{If } a_j < F \text{ then } (o_j) = 0$$

Step 2 is repeated for 10 cycles. If the parameters E and G are correctly adjusted then one unit in L2 will be maximally activated with the activation of other units in the competitive cluster tending towards zero.

Step 3: Update the weights

The weights (W_{ij}) on connections between the active unit in L2 and the input unit (a_i) are updated using either the Stent-Singer rule or the Rumelhart and Zipser normalization procedure.

$$W_{ij} = \Delta W_{ij} + W_{ij}$$

The Stent-Singer rule: If the input unit is active then the weight at the connection is increased by a proportion (A) of the output of the L2 unit.(A is specified by the parameter *Wt Inc* in the program).

$$\Delta W_{ij} = Ao_j$$

If the input unit is inactive then the weight is decreased by a proportion (B) of the output (B is specified by the parameter *Wt Dec* in the program).

$$\Delta W_{ij} = Bo_j$$

The Rumelhart and Zipser normalization procedure: Note that for this rule the total value of the summed weights between the input units in L1 and each unit in L2 are equal to 1. Each weight on connections between the input units and the winning unit unit in L2 is decremented by a proportion (G) of its own value. The sum of these decrements is then distributed equally to those weights on connections with active input units (a_i) only (n = number of active units).

$$\Delta W_{ij} = G\,(C/n) - GW_{ij}$$

$$C = 1 \quad \text{if } a_i > 0$$
$$C = 0 \quad \text{if } a_i = 0$$

The next pattern is presented to the net and the procedure starts again.

Author index

Subject Index

Contacting the authors

If you have any questions or comments regarding the Beginner's Guide, please contact:

Dr. Gerry Orchard
Cognitive and Computational Modelling Group
School of Psychology
10 Lennoxvale
Belfast
BT9 5BY

Gerry Orchard can also be contacted by Fax (Belfast 664144) or by E-mail (g.orchard@uk.ac.qub.v1). If you prefer to telephone, call Belfast 245133, ext 4354/4360.